Hamas

Understanding a Controversial Organization

Ashu Dhyani

FANTABULOUS
www.fantabulous.co.in

Publisher

Fantabulous Publishers India

www.fantabulous.co.in

Edition

2023

Hamas: Understanding a Controversial Organization

Penned by Ashu Dhyani

Published by Fantabulous Publishers India

Preface

Welcome to a journey into the heart of one of the most complex and controversial organizations in the modern world—Hamas. In this book, we embark on a quest to understand the multifaceted nature of an entity that has been both a symbol of resistance and a source of intense debate.

"Hamas: Understanding a Controversial Organization" is not a mere exploration of events; it is an invitation to navigate the nuances, challenge assumptions, and unravel the layers that shroud this organization. As we delve into its history, ideologies, and actions, we encounter a narrative that transcends the confines of the Israeli-Palestinian conflict.

This is not a black-and-white story. It's a tapestry woven with threads of political strategy, armed resistance, and the aspirations of a people under occupation. The controversies surrounding Hamas extend beyond borders, echoing in international discussions on terrorism, statehood, and the complexities of the Middle East.

Through brief profiles, timelines, and interviews, we aim to present a comprehensive view. We meet the architects of Hamas, delve into key events, and hear from voices that shape the organization's trajectory. It's an exploration that balances between the geopolitical realities and the human dimensions of the conflict.

But why should you care about Hamas? Because understanding this organization means delving into the heart of a conflict that has far-reaching implications. It means engaging with the challenges of governance in Gaza, the dynamics of resistance, and the persistent pursuit of justice and statehood.

As you flip through these pages, keep in mind that this book is not about taking sides. It's about fostering comprehension. Whether you're well-versed in the region's history or approaching it for the first time, our goal is to offer clarity amid the controversy.

So, fasten your seatbelt. This is not a passive reading experience; it's an active journey into understanding. Through the controversies and complexities, we invite you to join us in peeling back the layers and gaining insight into the enigma that is Hamas.

Ashu Dhyani.

Contents

Hamas

Understanding a Controversial Organization

Chapter 1: Introduction

As we plunge into the labyrinth of the Israeli-Palestinian saga, there exists a name that reverberates with both intrigue and controversy—Hamas. The mere mention of this enigmatic entity conjures up images of resistance, conflict, and an unwavering commitment that has left an indelible mark on the volatile canvas of the Middle East.

Amidst the perpetual backdrop of the Israeli-Palestinian clash, Hamas emerges as a central figure, its role both pivotal and polarizing. Forged in the crucible of political turbulence within the Palestinian territories, it has evolved into a multifaceted force, wielding influence that ripples across the region. Consider this chapter your invitation into the captivating world of Hamas—a sneak peek into its inner workings, a glimpse at its historical roots, and an exploration of its delicate dance as both a political powerhouse and a formidable militant force.

However, to truly grasp the complexities of Hamas and its role in the ongoing drama, let's rewind the clock to its origin— a time when the Palestinian territories were alive with the fervor of protest, rebellion, and an impassioned call for self-determination.

1.1a The Genesis of Hamas

As the night draped its mysterious cloak over the Al-Shati refugee camp on December 9, 1987, an unassuming house became the clandestine stage for an event that would alter the course of Palestinian history. Sheikh Ahmad Yassin, a paraplegic luminary with a flowing white beard and a reputation for visionary wisdom, took center stage in this clandestine gathering. The walls of Shati, haunted by the collective memories of dispossession, bore witness to a chapter yet unwritten.

Amidst the flickering shadows, Yassin, the host and inadvertent harbinger of change, welcomed a diverse assembly of attendees—refugees, like himself, from towns and villages swallowed by the ever-expanding borders of Israel. Their urgency was palpable, a shared sense of displacement and a pressing need to make sense of the swirling events around them.

In the intimate quarters of that humble abode, the air crackled with anticipation. The gathering was more than a convergence of individuals; it was a collective pilgrimage to redefine the Palestinian narrative. Against the backdrop of Shati's narrow alleyways and the haunting tales of a dispersed people, the embryonic seeds of what would become Hamas found fertile ground.

The scene was set, and the walls whispered witness to the birth pangs of a movement. Sheikh Ahmad Yassin, in his visionary stature, inadvertently laid the cornerstone for an entity that would navigate the labyrinth of Palestinian identity and resistance. Unbeknownst to those present, the narrative of that night would not be confined to the Shati refugee camp. It would resonate through the decades, shaping the very contours of a story that continues to unfold against the complex backdrop of the Middle East. The genesis of Hamas, a chapter yet untold, had begun.

In the late 1980s, amidst the tumult of the Israeli-Palestinian conflict, Hamas, derived from the Arabic acronym "Harakat al-Muqawamah al-Islamiyyah" or the Islamic Resistance Movement, officially came into existence. The backdrop was the First Intifada, a period when the Palestinian territories resonated with protests, uprisings, and a fervent call for independence. In this cauldron of unrest, Hamas found its raison d'être.

Born as a response to the perceived shortcomings of existing Palestinian political entities, Hamas, led by visionaries like Sheikh Ahmed Yassin and Abdel Aziz al-Rantisi, aimed to fill the void. Their vision was a unique blend of religious devotion and political resistance, with the overarching goal of countering Israeli occupation and ultimately establishing an Islamic state in historic Palestine.

1.1b The First Intifada: Seeds of Dissent

The First Intifada, or "Uprising," that burst into life in December 1987 was a turning point in the Israeli-Palestinian conflict. It was an organic and largely grassroots Palestinian uprising, characterized by its spontaneity and a genuine expression of the people's collective desire for independence and an end to the perceived Israeli oppression that had cast a long shadow over their lives.

The Intifada, which means "shaking off" in Arabic, was a manifestation of the deep-seated grievances that had festered among Palestinians for years. In a landscape marred by military checkpoints, restricted movement, and economic hardship, a spark was all that was needed to ignite this conflagration of discontent.

During this tumultuous period, a wide range of political and social movements emerged, each vying to represent the Palestinian cause. These included the Palestine Liberation Organization (PLO), Fatah, and a host of other factions. Yet, among this mosaic of resistance, Hamas found its niche and its raison d'être.

Life in the occupied Palestinian territories had become increasingly difficult, with the restrictions imposed by Israeli military occupation creating a pressure cooker of frustration and resentment. It was within this cauldron of unrest that the First Intifada was born.

The spark that ignited the Intifada came in the form of a tragic traffic accident. On December 8, 1987, an Israeli truck collided with a vehicle carrying Palestinian laborers, resulting in the deaths of four Palestinians in the Gaza Strip. The incident quickly became a focal point for widespread anger and frustration.

The spontaneous outpouring of grief and rage was akin to a dam bursting, as Palestinians, both young and old, poured into the streets, fueling a rapidly growing movement. Protests, strikes, and demonstrations quickly spread, transcending geographical and demographic boundaries.

The heart of the Intifada was a yearning for self-determination and an end to Israeli occupation. Palestinians had witnessed the peace process, encapsulated in the Oslo Accords, stagnate without delivering the promised resolution to their plight. They had endured years of subjugation, displacement, and loss, and they saw the First Intifada as a genuine, grassroots expression of their desire for freedom and sovereignty.

Palestinians from all walks of life, from students to workers to families, took part in the uprising. Young people, in particular, played a significant role, hurling stones and molotov cocktails at Israeli soldiers, becoming the iconic face of the Intifada. They, too, had known little else but occupation, curfews, and checkpoints.

What further distinguished the First Intifada was the emergence of a diverse mosaic of political and social movements, each striving to represent the Palestinian cause. In this period of fervor and political awakening, existing factions such as the Palestine Liberation Organization (PLO), led by Yasser Arafat, and Fatah, the dominant faction within the PLO, continued to exert their influence.

However, the Intifada opened the door to new voices in the Palestinian struggle. Among them was Hamas, which found fertile ground for its message of combining religious devotion with political resistance. Hamas's founders believed that this combination could offer a unique approach to the Israeli-Palestinian conflict.

To understand Hamas's genesis within the First Intifada, we must also acknowledge the suffering of the Palestinian people. Their pain was palpable and found expression in the Intifada's fervent call for justice. The desire for independence was not an abstract concept; it was a visceral need for a generation that had grown up knowing little else but conflict and occupation.

Countless Palestinians had experienced the loss of loved ones, seen their homes demolished, or felt the daily humiliation of living under Israeli military rule. The First Intifada became a collective catharsis, a cry for freedom, justice, and the reclamation of their stolen dignity.

1.1c A Religious Response

Hamas set itself apart from the existing political factions by intertwining its struggle for Palestinian independence with a deeply rooted Islamist ideology. Founded by individuals such as Sheikh Ahmed Yassin and Abdel Aziz al-Rantisi, Hamas aimed to offer a unique blend of Islamic devotion and political resistance. Its message resonated with a segment of the Palestinian population that sought a more religiously grounded approach to the conflict.

At its core, Hamas viewed the Israeli-Palestinian conflict through a religious lens. The organization's founding charter, published in 1988, expressed its commitment to the establishment of an Islamic state in historic Palestine, encompassing present-day Israel, the West Bank, and the Gaza

Strip. This vision was fundamentally different from the secular nationalist approach advocated by the PLO and Fatah.

Hamas's charter contained elements of anti-Semitism and rejected the legitimacy of the State of Israel. Its ideology viewed the struggle against Israeli occupation as a religious duty, and it justified the use of violence to achieve its goals.

At its core, Hamas's identity was deeply intertwined with the Islamic faith. This distinctive fusion of religion and political resistance was an intrinsic part of the organization's character. It aimed to create a unique narrative that framed the Israeli-Palestinian conflict through a religious lens, asserting that their struggle was not merely a political one, but a divine duty.

The leaders of Hamas believed that by grounding their resistance in religious principles, they could rally support from segments of the Palestinian population who sought a more faith-based approach to the conflict. In doing so, they offered an alternative to the secular nationalist approach advocated by the Palestine Liberation Organization (PLO) and its dominant faction, Fatah.

Hamas's commitment to its religious ideology was clearly articulated in its founding charter, published in 1988. This foundational document expressed the organization's dedication to establishing an Islamic state in historic Palestine, encompassing not only the occupied territories but also present-day Israel. The vision outlined in this charter was fundamentally different from the goals of the PLO and Fatah, which sought a secular Palestinian state alongside Israel.

This vision of an Islamic state encompassing the entirety of historic Palestine has been a source of tension, not only with Israel but also with other Palestinian political factions. The idea of an Islamic state, where religious principles and laws govern society, has generated apprehension among some Palestinians who have a more secular or moderate outlook.

In addition to its vision of an Islamic state, Hamas's charter contained elements that have drawn international scrutiny and condemnation. The document included statements that were perceived as anti-Semitic and hostile to the State of Israel. Such rhetoric has fueled concerns and contributed to Hamas's status as a terrorist organization in the eyes of various countries.

One of the most controversial aspects of Hamas's ideology was its justification for the use of violence as a means to achieve its goals. The charter portrayed the struggle against Israeli occupation as a religious duty, effectively sanctioning the use of force in the pursuit of Palestinian independence. This stance has underpinned the organization's militant activities, including suicide bombings, rocket attacks, and other acts of violence.

In examining Hamas's religious response to the Israeli-Palestinian conflict, it's essential to consider the broader context of Palestinian aspirations and frustrations. For many

Palestinians, the conflict has resulted in immeasurable suffering—displacement, loss of life, and a sense of enduring injustice. It is within this cauldron of emotions and experiences that Hamas found fertile ground for its message.

The pain and loss experienced by Palestinians over decades have forged a deep-seated desire for justice, self-determination, and the reclamation of their stolen dignity. It is a sentiment that goes beyond politics; it's a cry for the restoration of their human rights and freedom. The message offered by Hamas, rooted in religious devotion and a commitment to resistance, resonated with a segment of the Palestinian population who felt that their struggle was, at its core, a spiritual one.

1.1d The Birth of a Resistance Movement

During the early stages of the First Intifada, Hamas, like many other Palestinian factions, engaged in acts of civil disobedience to voice its grievances and challenge the Israeli occupation. Strikes, boycotts, and mass protests became the norm, as Palestinians sought to make their presence felt and their demands known.

However, what set Hamas apart was its willingness to escalate its resistance to armed actions against Israeli military targets and civilians. This transformation, driven by its deeply rooted Islamist ideology, marked a turning point in the Intifada.

Hamas's armed wing, known as the Izz ad-Din al-Qassam Brigades, became the face of its militancy. The brigades were responsible for conducting attacks against Israeli forces, and it was during this period that tactics such as suicide bombings and rocket launches became synonymous with Hamas. These acts of violence, often directed at civilian targets, generated both fear and outrage, catapulting Hamas into the international spotlight.

As the First Intifada continued to unfold, Hamas's influence and popularity grew, particularly in the Gaza Strip. The organization's appeal resonated deeply with segments of the population who had long endured the harsh realities of life under Israeli occupation.

Gaza, with its dense population and history of suffering, became a focal point of Hamas's rise. The territory's residents had experienced economic hardship, restrictions on their movement, and the consequences of repeated conflicts. In this environment, Hamas's message of resistance and a faith-based approach found receptive ears.

Hamas's growth in popularity was not solely a result of its militant activities. The organization extended its reach by providing essential social services and welfare programs to

Palestinians in need. This comprehensive approach encompassed education, healthcare, and other vital services. Hamas established schools, hospitals, and charitable foundations to support the local community.

These initiatives were not mere charity work; they created a social safety net for Palestinians in Gaza, a region heavily impacted by the strains of occupation. For many, these services offered a lifeline, and Hamas, by providing them, established a strong presence in the hearts and minds of the people.

1.1e Founding Principles

Hamas is designated as a terrorist organization by several countries and entities, including the United States, the European Union, Israel, and others. It's important to note that this designation can vary by region and perspective, and some parties may not consider Hamas a terrorist organization. However, for the purpose of this book, we will provide an overview of its principles and ideology.

1. **Armed Resistance:** Hamas is committed to armed resistance against Israeli occupation. This includes the use of force, including acts of violence and terrorism, as a means to

achieve its goals. The organization views this resistance as a legitimate response to Israeli actions in the Palestinian territories.

2. **Islamic Ideology:** At its core, Hamas is deeply intertwined with Islamic ideology. Its mission is not only political but also religious in nature. The organization seeks to establish an Islamic state in historic Palestine, encompassing present-day Israel, the West Bank, and the Gaza Strip. This sets it apart from other Palestinian political factions that follow a more secular nationalist approach.

3. **Founding Figures:** Key figures like Sheikh Ahmed Yassin and Abdel Aziz al-Rantisi were instrumental in shaping Hamas's ideology. They played significant roles in articulating the organization's vision and garnering support from the Palestinian population.

4. **Rejection of the State of Israel:** Hamas's founding charter contains elements of anti-Semitism and rejects the legitimacy of the State of Israel. It views the Israeli-Palestinian conflict through a religious lens, justifying its struggle as a religious duty.

5. **Use of Violence:** Hamas justifies the use of violence as a means to achieve its goals, including suicide bombings, rocket attacks, and other forms of violence. This approach has drawn both support and condemnation, making it a highly controversial aspect of the organization.

Understanding these founding principles is crucial to comprehending Hamas's objectives and actions in the context of the Israeli-Palestinian conflict. While some view Hamas as a legitimate resistance movement, others consider it a terrorist organization due to its methods and goals.

Initial Take:

The genesis of Hamas is a story of a grassroots movement that rose to prominence in the tumultuous climate of the First Intifada. Founded on a deeply rooted Islamist ideology, Hamas sought to offer a unique blend of religious devotion and political resistance, framing the Israeli-Palestinian conflict within a religious context. This set it apart from other Palestinian factions, such as the PLO and Fatah, and drew it a following among those who sought a more faith-based approach to the struggle for Palestinian independence.

1.2. The Dual Nature of Hamas

One of the defining features of Hamas is its dual identity. It operates as both a political and a militant organization, which makes it a complex and often polarizing entity. This strategy is designed to protect the rights of Palestinians against Israeli ambitions. While the political wing of Hamas tends to face less criticism, its military activities raise deeper concerns, particularly regarding the use of force in pursuit of its goals. This duality adds to the complexity of how Hamas is viewed.

1.2a. Political Face:

Hamas participates in Palestinian politics, primarily through its engagement in legislative elections and governance. The organization won a decisive victory in the 2006 Palestinian legislative elections, gaining a majority of seats in the Palestinian Legislative Council. It secured 74 out of 132 seats, defying the expectations of many and becoming the dominant political force in the Palestinian territories. The success of Hamas in these elections marked a seismic shift in the region, ushering in a period of political change and turbulence.

Hamas's victory in the legislative elections meant that it would be tasked with governing the Palestinian territories. This governance primarily took shape in the Gaza Strip, where Hamas assumed control, leading to the establishment of a de facto authority. The West Bank, under the leadership of the Fatah-dominated Palestinian Authority led by President Mahmoud Abbas, remained under different political control. This division between the West Bank and Gaza Strip has persisted, creating a complex political dynamic that continues to impact the Palestinian territories.

Hamas's involvement in Palestinian politics goes beyond its role in governance. The organization extends its reach into the provision of social services to Palestinian communities, with a particular focus on the Gaza Strip. These services play a crucial role in the daily lives of Palestinians living in the territory.

Hamas runs schools, hospitals, and welfare programs, creating a comprehensive social safety net for the population. This multifaceted approach to governance and social services reflects the organization's commitment to addressing the pressing needs of the Palestinian people.

The educational and healthcare institutions managed by Hamas serve not only as a response to the challenges posed by the ongoing conflict but also as a symbol of resilience. In a region often marked by economic hardship, political instability, and the consequences of repeated conflicts, these services have proven invaluable.

The schools provide education for Palestinian children, offering a glimmer of hope for a brighter future despite the adversity they face. The hospitals offer essential medical care, often in an environment where access to healthcare can be limited. Welfare programs offer support to those in need, mitigating the impact of economic hardship and ensuring that the most vulnerable are not left behind.

The provision of social services has earned Hamas a degree of popular support among the local population. To many Palestinians in Gaza, these services represent not only a lifeline but also a form of steadfast resistance, as they continue to live in the shadow of an unresolved conflict.

1.2b. Militant Wing:

In parallel with its political activities, Hamas has a militant wing that conducts armed resistance against Israeli forces. This wing, known as the Izz ad-Din al-Qassam Brigades, is responsible for launching attacks, including suicide bombings, rocket fire, and other acts of violence. This dual nature, being both a political player and a militant force, has been a source of considerable controversy and conflict.

In the intricate tapestry of the Israeli-Palestinian conflict, Hamas's militant activities have earned it both international notoriety and a complex, often contentious, role in the region. The Izz ad-Din al-Qassam Brigades, often simply referred to as the al-Qassam Brigades, serve as Hamas's military wing. Named after Izz ad-Din al-Qassam, a Syrian preacher and early leader of Palestinian resistance against the British Mandate and Zionist settlements in the early 20th century, these brigades are the armed face of Hamas. They are entrusted with the responsibility of conducting armed resistance against Israeli forces and pursuing the broader goals of the organization.

The al-Qassam Brigades employ various methods of armed resistance in their struggle against Israeli forces. One of the most controversial and well-known tactics is suicide bombings. These attacks have targeted not only military installations but also civilian areas, leading to significant loss of life and injuries. Suicide bombings, in particular, have sparked widespread condemnation and have been a point of contention in the Israeli-Palestinian conflict.

Rocket attacks, including firing rockets into Israeli territory, have also been a hallmark of the al-Qassam Brigades' activities. These attacks, often indiscriminate in nature, have resulted in damage to property and, at times, casualties among the Israeli civilian population. The use of such weaponry has been a source of international concern and a catalyst for periodic escalations of violence in the region.

Other forms of violence, including clashes with Israeli forces, have characterized the activities of the al-Qassam Brigades. These confrontations, sometimes resulting in casualties on both sides, further underscore the high-stakes nature of the Israeli-Palestinian conflict.

This is a significant issue in the region, further complicating the situation. Hamas's choice of military action and violence has overshadowed their social efforts in Gaza, leading to a negative international response. The world has responded to Hamas's actions in various ways. While some nations, particularly in the Middle East, have expressed support for the Palestinian cause, many countries and international organizations have condemned Hamas's use of violence and its tactics, such as rocket attacks and suicide bombings.

Hamas's attacks have had a significant impact on Israel. Israeli civilians have suffered injuries and loss of life due to suicide bombings and rocket attacks. The constant threat of rocket fire from Gaza has forced Israeli communities near the border to live under the shadow of potential violence.

However, the actions of Hamas have also impacted the Palestinian territories. Israeli military responses to Hamas attacks, particularly in densely populated areas like the Gaza Strip, have led to Palestinian casualties and destruction of infrastructure. The cycle of violence has perpetuated suffering among the Palestinian population.

Numerous peace initiatives and negotiations have been attempted to address the Israeli-Palestinian conflict, with the aim of achieving a two-state solution. However, the actions of Hamas and the broader conflict dynamics have made reaching a lasting peace agreement challenging.

However, in current international scenario, Hamas is designated as a terrorist organization by several countries, including the United States, Israel, the European Union, and others, due to its use of violence and armed resistance in the context of the Israeli-Palestinian conflict. The international community often calls for a cessation of violence and a peaceful resolution to the ongoing conflict.

"Below are some of the significant methods of violence taken by Hamas:"

1. Suicide Bombings:

In the early 2000s, Hamas was responsible for a series of suicide bombings in Israel. These attacks targeted buses, cafes, and other public places, resulting in numerous casualties among Israeli civilians. The era of suicide bombings represents a dark chapter in the history of the Israeli-Palestinian conflict. The actions of Hamas during this period remain a subject of intense debate, as they continue to influence the dynamics of the ongoing conflict and shape international responses to the organization.

The international community responded to these suicide bombings with condemnation and concern. The deliberate targeting of civilians, regardless of their nationality, was widely regarded as a breach of fundamental principles of humanity and international law.

Hamas's tactics, including suicide bombings, led to its designation as a terrorist organization by many countries, and this status was reinforced by its actions during this period.

Efforts to address the Israeli-Palestinian conflict, negotiate ceasefires, and pursue peace initiatives were further complicated by the cycle of violence triggered by these bombings.

Below are just a few examples, and there have been several more suicide bombings attributed to Hamas over the years.

Sbarro Pizzeria Bombing (2001): In August 2001, a suicide bomber walked into the Sbarro Pizzeria in Jerusalem and detonated a bomb, killing 15 people, including 7 children, and injuring over 100 others. Hamas claimed responsibility for this attack.

Dolphinarium Discotheque (2001): In June 2001, a suicide bomber targeted the Dolphinarium discotheque in Tel Aviv. The attack resulted in the deaths of 21 people, most of them teenagers, and left dozens injured. Hamas claimed responsibility for this devastating act.

Passover Massacre (2002): In March 2002, a suicide bomber targeted a Passover Seder in a hotel in Netanya, Israel. The attack resulted in 30 deaths and numerous injuries. Hamas also claimed responsibility for this bombing.

Kiryat HaYovel supermarket bombing (2002): In March 2002, a suicide bomber attacked a supermarket in Jerusalem's Kiryat HaYovel neighborhood. The explosion killed two people and wounded dozens. Hamas claimed responsibility for this bombing.

Egged Bus 32A (2002): In March 2002, a suicide bomber blew up an Egged bus in Haifa, killing 17 people and injuring over 40. Hamas claimed responsibility for this attack as well.

2. Rocket Attacks:

Hamas has frequently fired rockets from the Gaza Strip into Israeli territory. These rocket attacks have caused damage to homes, infrastructure, and have led to injuries and loss of life among Israeli civilians. Some examples of Rocket attacks are mentioned below…

- (a) **Gaza War (2008-2009):** During the Gaza War, also known as Operation Cast Lead, Hamas fired numerous rockets into southern Israel. The conflict, which began in December 2008 and lasted for several weeks, resulted in significant rocket attacks from Gaza, leading to casualties and damage in Israeli towns and cities. The conflict showcased the vulnerability of civilian populations in the midst of political and military strife.

In response to the rocket attacks, Israel initiated Operation Cast Lead, a military offensive aimed at dismantling Hamas's infrastructure and curtailing its ability to launch further attacks.

The conflict witnessed a series of strategic maneuvers and counter-maneuvers, as both sides sought to gain the upper hand. Hamas, deeply entrenched in the densely populated Gaza Strip, employed guerrilla tactics and embedded its military infrastructure within civilian areas, complicating Israeli military efforts and drawing international condemnation.

Losses were felt on both sides, with casualties among civilians and combatants. The conflict's toll extended beyond the immediate physical damage, leaving a lasting impact on the psychological and political landscape of the region. Interviews with leaders and representatives from both sides provided insights into their perspectives, revealing the complex motivations driving the conflict.

- **(b) Operation Pillar of Defense (2012): Operation Pillar of Defense Unleashes Eight-Day Clash in 2012**

In a dramatic escalation of tensions, November 2012 saw the eruption of Operation Pillar of Defense, a high-stakes conflict between Israel and militant factions in Gaza. The catalyst for this eight-day clash was the targeted Israeli airstrike that eliminated Ahmed Jabari, a key figure in the Hamas military leadership.

The tumultuous events unfolded as Hamas and other militant groups in Gaza unleashed a relentless barrage of rockets, propelling the region into a state of chaos. The strike on Jabari, seen as a pivotal figure in Hamas' military apparatus, marked a strategic move by Israel to cripple the organization's command structure.

The conflict quickly spiraled into a full-scale confrontation, characterized by intense fighting and strategic maneuvers on both sides. Israeli forces implemented a range of tactics aimed at neutralizing rocket launch sites in Gaza, while Gaza-based militants persisted with their assault on southern Israel.

Casualties mounted, and both sides endured significant damage, with civilian populations caught in the crossfire. The conflict's toll was felt not only in the physical destruction but also in the emotional strain on affected communities.

Amid the chaos, interviews with civilians on both sides offered a glimpse into the human impact of the conflict. Families huddled in bomb shelters, recounting harrowing tales of survival, while others mourned the loss of loved ones. In the streets of Gaza and southern Israel, the fear and uncertainty were palpable.

As the conflict unfolded, political leaders and military officials on both sides engaged in a war of words, just as their forces clashed on the ground. The international community watched with growing concern, calling for an immediate ceasefire to prevent further escalation.

Ultimately, after eight days of intense hostilities, a ceasefire brokered by Egypt brought a temporary halt to the fighting. The aftermath left a region scarred by the physical and emotional toll of Operation Pillar of Defense, prompting renewed international efforts to address the underlying issues fueling the Israeli-Palestinian conflict.

- (c) Operation Protective Edge Unleashes 50 Days of Conflict in 2014

In a tumultuous July of 2014, Operation Protective Edge thrust the Israeli-Palestinian conflict into the global spotlight, marking a 50-day period of intense hostilities. The catalyst for this prolonged clash was the relentless barrage of rockets launched by Hamas into Israeli territory.

The conflict began with Hamas firing thousands of rockets indiscriminately, causing fear and chaos among Israeli civilians. In response, Israeli forces swiftly implemented a multifaceted strategy, combining precision airstrikes with a ground incursion into Gaza. The aim was to dismantle Hamas' military infrastructure and neutralize the threat posed by the rocket attacks.

As the conflict unfolded, both sides engaged in a complex dance of military strategies. Israeli forces meticulously targeted rocket launch sites and militant strongholds, while Hamas employed guerrilla tactics and embedded themselves within civilian areas, intensifying the challenges faced by the Israeli military.

The toll of Operation Protective Edge was devastating, with civilian casualties on both sides. The international community responded with grave concern as scenes of destruction and human suffering dominated headlines. Interviews with those directly affected painted a vivid picture of the human cost of the conflict, with families torn apart and communities shattered.

Losses were not confined to physical infrastructure; the conflict also took a toll on diplomatic relations. The international response ranged from calls for an immediate ceasefire to condemnations and expressions of solidarity with the affected populations.

After 50 days of relentless fighting, a ceasefire brokered by regional and international actors brought a temporary halt to the hostilities. The aftermath left a scarred landscape in both Gaza and Israel, prompting renewed calls for a comprehensive and lasting resolution to the longstanding Israeli-Palestinian conflict.

- **(d) Operation Protective Edge (2018) Ignites New Confrontation**

In a stark resurgence of hostilities, July 2018 witnessed the eruption of Operation Protective Edge, a clash between Hamas and other militant factions in Gaza, and the Israeli military. The conflict unfolded as Hamas and its counterparts fired a barrage of rockets into southern Israel, triggering a swift and forceful response from the Israeli forces.

The exchange of rocket fire set off a series of events that reverberated across the region. Israel, determined to protect its citizens from the indiscriminate attacks, launched a series of precision airstrikes targeting militant positions in Gaza. The strategic moves aimed to degrade the capabilities of the armed groups responsible for the rocket attacks.

The volatile situation led to casualties and significant damage on both sides, as civilian populations found themselves caught in the crossfire. The toll of Operation Protective Edge was not confined to physical destruction; it also manifested in the emotional strain on affected communities.

In the aftermath of the clashes, interviews with civilians on both sides provided a poignant insight into the human impact of the conflict. Families in southern Israel sought refuge in bomb shelters, recounting tales of fear and resilience, while those in Gaza grappled with the challenges of daily life amid the turmoil.

The international community closely monitored the events, expressing concern over the escalating violence. Calls for restraint and diplomatic solutions echoed on the global stage as leaders sought to prevent further escalation and mitigate the human suffering caused by the conflict.

Operation Protective Edge, with its complexities and repercussions, underscored the enduring challenges in the Israeli-Palestinian conflict. As the region grappled with the aftermath, the quest for a lasting and comprehensive resolution remained a pressing concern.

- **(e) May 2021 Escalation: Rockets Rain Down on Israeli Cities**

In a tense and volatile turn of events in May 2021, the Israeli-Palestinian conflict reached a boiling point when Hamas unleashed a barrage of rockets into Israeli cities and towns, including the highly populated areas of Jerusalem and Tel Aviv. The immediate catalyst for this escalation was the mounting tensions in East Jerusalem, adding fuel to an already volatile situation.

The rocket attacks from Hamas led to a harrowing reality for Israeli civilians, causing injuries and extensive damage to critical infrastructure. With sirens blaring and residents seeking refuge in bomb shelters, the conflict unfolded in the heart of densely populated urban centers.

Israel responded with a series of precision airstrikes in Gaza, employing a strategic approach aimed at dismantling Hamas's military capabilities and neutralizing the immediate threat posed by the rocket attacks. The military strategies on both sides unfolded in the midst of a complex and charged geopolitical landscape.

The toll of the conflict was not only measured in physical damage but also in human suffering. Interviews with those directly affected provided a poignant glimpse into the emotional impact of the events. Families grappling with the trauma of living under the threat of rocket attacks and airstrikes shared their stories, highlighting the profound human cost of the conflict.

As international concern grew, diplomatic efforts were mobilized to bring about a ceasefire and address the underlying issues that fueled the cycle of violence. The May 2021 conflict, with its rapid and intense escalation, underscored the fragility of the situation in the region and the urgent need for a comprehensive and lasting resolution to the Israeli-Palestinian conflict.

- **(f) Ongoing Cross-Border Tensions Unleash Sporadic Violence in 2023**

In the continuing saga of the Israeli-Palestinian conflict, 2023 has witnessed a familiar but troubling trend – sporadic rocket attacks launched by Hamas into Israeli territory. Despite lacking the formal categorization of a specific operation, these incursions have played a pivotal role in sustaining the atmosphere of unrest in the region.

The recurring rocket attacks, originating from Hamas, have become a regrettable hallmark of this enduring conflict. The consequences are not limited to the immediate threat they pose to Israeli civilians; they also set in motion a well-practiced sequence of events. In response, Israel has consistently executed retaliatory airstrikes, implementing strategic measures to counteract the threat and safeguard its populace.

The toll of this ongoing skirmish is not only measured in physical terms. Injuries and property damage on both sides serve as stark reminders of the human cost and the lasting impact on affected communities. Interviews with individuals living through these turbulent times provide poignant insights into the daily challenges faced by those caught in the crossfire.

As the conflict persists, the absence of a designated operation does not diminish the urgency of the situation. The cyclical nature of these cross-border attacks underscores the deeply rooted complexities of the Israeli-Palestinian conflict. While diplomatic efforts continue, the pressing need for a sustainable resolution remains paramount, as communities on both sides grapple with the enduring consequences of these periodic bursts of violence.

These examples highlight the devastating impact of Hamas's suicide bombings on both Israeli civilians and the broader dynamics of the Israeli-Palestinian conflict. These attacks have led to significant loss of life and injury, leaving a lasting mark on the history of the region.

3. Hamas' Intricate Tunnel Network

In a strategic move that has escalated tensions in the region, Hamas, the militant group controlling the Gaza Strip, has meticulously constructed a network of tunnels beneath the enclave's surface. These subterranean passages, some extending into Israeli territory, serve a multi-faceted purpose, marking a significant chapter in the ongoing Israeli-Palestinian conflict.

The tunnels, a testament to Hamas' resourcefulness, have been employed for various nefarious activities. Notably, they have been utilized for the clandestine smuggling of weapons, amplifying the threat posed by the militant group. Furthermore, these covert passages have become launch points for attacks against both Israeli soldiers and civilians, highlighting the brazen nature of Hamas' tactics.

The revelation of this subterranean network has underscored the complexity of the conflict, with Hamas employing underground infrastructure as a strategic tool. The Israeli military, cognizant of the threat posed by these tunnels, has responded with counter-strategies aimed at detecting and neutralizing these hidden passages.

The toll of this subterranean warfare is not confined to military engagements; it resonates with civilians on both sides. Interviews with those directly affected shed light on the fear and uncertainty that accompany the awareness of tunnels beneath their feet. Families living in proximity to these covert structures face a heightened sense of vulnerability, emphasizing the profound impact of Hamas' tactics on daily life in the region.

As this subterranean chapter unfolds, it adds a new layer of complexity to the protracted conflict, requiring strategic adaptations and an ongoing commitment to safeguarding the security and well-being of all those caught in its web.

4. Border Protests: Hamas has organized and participated in protests at the Gaza-Israel border. While many of these protests have been non-violent, some have escalated into clashes with Israeli forces, resulting in casualties.

The Controversial Duality

Hamas's dual identity as both a political entity and a militant force has been a wellspring of controversy. The coexistence of these two faces within a single organization has generated significant debate, both regionally and internationally.

On one hand, Hamas's participation in Palestinian politics and governance has led to its recognition as a legitimate representative of the Palestinian people by some nations and entities. Its electoral victories have conferred a degree of political legitimacy, particularly in the Gaza Strip. The social services it provides have also garnered local support.

On the other hand, the al-Qassam Brigades' armed actions have raised considerable concerns. Suicide bombings and rocket attacks have been widely condemned for their impact on civilian populations and their potential to derail peace efforts. The international community, including many Western countries, has designated the al-Qassam Brigades as a terrorist organization.

The dual nature of Hamas, a duality encompassing political representation and armed resistance, has, in essence, created a dichotomy in how it is viewed and engaged with on the global stage. The complexity of this situation is a reflection of the broader complexities of the Israeli-Palestinian conflict, where narratives, perspectives, and solutions are far from one-dimensional.

1.3. International Perspectives on Hamas

Understanding Hamas requires a nuanced perspective, especially when it comes to its international standing. Different countries and organizations view Hamas in diverse ways, which contributes to its contentious status on the global stage.

1. Terrorist Organization Designation: A significant number of countries, including the United States, Israel, the European Union, and others, classify Hamas as a terrorist organization. This designation is primarily due to the group's use of violence, including suicide bombings and rocket attacks, against civilian targets.

2. Regional Support: On the flip side, there are nations and groups, most notably Iran and some Arab states, that provide political and financial support to Hamas. They see the organization as a legitimate resistance movement fighting against Israeli occupation.

3. Mixed International Recognition: Some countries and international bodies, such as the United Nations, have a more nuanced approach. While recognizing the need for a peaceful resolution to the Israeli-Palestinian conflict, they have engaged with Hamas in certain capacities, especially in the realm of humanitarian aid and ceasefire negotiations.

1.4. The Complex Reality of Hamas

As we delve into this exploration of Hamas, it is essential to recognize the complex reality of this organization. Hamas is neither a monolithic entity nor a simple force for good or evil.

Instead, it operates within a web of historical, political, and social factors that have shaped its evolution.

This book aims to provide an in-depth understanding of Hamas, examining its history, ideology, goals, and the controversies that surround it. While acknowledging its designation as a terrorist organization by various governments, we will also explore the impact of Hamas on the Palestinian territories and the broader Middle East.

Chapter 2: Hamas Strategies and Attacks

Hamas, as an organization, employs a multifaceted strategy in its approach towards Israel. At the core of its strategy is the use of armed resistance to challenge Israeli occupation and to advance its vision of establishing an Islamic state in historic Palestine, which includes present-day Israel, the West Bank, and the Gaza Strip. This approach is characterized by the use of force, including acts of violence and terrorism, as a means to achieve its goals. Additionally, Hamas is known for launching rocket attacks into Israeli territory, aiming to disrupt normal life and challenge Israeli security measures. This strategy, which combines both political and military elements, has made Hamas a complex and polarizing entity in the Israeli-Palestinian conflict, with supporters viewing it as a legitimate resistance movement and critics categorizing it as a terrorist organization. Understanding Hamas's strategy is essential for comprehending its role and impact in this enduring and complex conflict.

Four major strategies that Hamas uses to attack Israeli military:

- Suicide Bimbing
- Rocket attack

- Tunnel strategy
- Border Protests

2.1 Suicide Bombing:

(i) Sbarro Pizzeria Bombing (2001) - A Tragic Day in Jerusalem

In the tumultuous history of the Israeli-Palestinian conflict, certain events stand out as harrowing reminders of the profound human cost and devastating impact of violence. The Sbarro Pizzeria bombing of August 2001 is one such tragedy, etched into the collective memory of those affected by the conflict and the international community alike.

The Prelude: Planning and Strategy

The planning and execution of the Sbarro Pizzeria bombing were part of a broader strategy employed by Hamas, the Islamic Resistance Movement, in its ongoing resistance against Israeli forces. The organization's tactics often included suicide bombings, with the objective of instilling fear, causing significant casualties among Israeli civilians, and amplifying its message of resistance.

In the case of the Sbarro attack, meticulous planning went into the operation. A suicide bomber was chosen, and the target - the Sbarro Pizzeria in the heart of Jerusalem - was carefully selected. The choice of a crowded restaurant during lunchtime was not coincidental. It was a deliberate attempt to maximize casualties and psychological impact.

The Day of Tragedy

On August 9, 2001, a suicide bomber, carrying an explosive device concealed in a guitar case, walked into the Sbarro Pizzeria in downtown Jerusalem. At the height of lunch hour, when the restaurant was bustling with customers, the bomber detonated the device, resulting in a massive explosion.

The immediate aftermath was a scene of chaos and devastation. The explosion shattered the restaurant, sending shards of glass, debris, and shrapnel flying in all directions. The impact was horrifying, and the consequences were heartbreaking.

Causalities and Impact

The Sbarro Pizzeria bombing left in its wake a devastating toll of casualties. Fifteen people lost their lives in the attack, including seven children. Over 100 others were injured, many of them severely. Families were shattered, and the shockwaves of the blast extended far beyond the immediate vicinity of the restaurant.

The tragedy was a stark reminder of the human cost of the Israeli-Palestinian conflict. It was a day that would forever haunt the survivors and the families of the victims, a day that punctuated the ongoing cycle of violence in the region.

Hamas's Claim of Responsibility

Hamas wasted no time in claiming responsibility for the Sbarro Pizzeria bombing. The organization regarded such acts as legitimate forms of resistance in the context of the conflict. Its leaders saw suicide bombings as a means to press their demands, to draw attention to the Palestinian cause, and to destabilize the Israeli population.

International Response and Designation as a Terrorist Organization

The international community reacted to the Sbarro bombing with condemnation. The deliberate targeting of civilians, including children, was widely regarded as an egregious breach of humanitarian and international laws. The attack further solidified the stance of many countries and entities in designating Hamas as a terrorist organization.

The Sbarro Pizzeria bombing, with its profound human toll and the global outrage it incited, became a symbol of the challenges and complexities of the Israeli-Palestinian conflict. It was a tragic day that underscored the urgent need for a resolution to the protracted conflict, a need that continues to be felt in the region and beyond.

(ii). Dolphinarium Discotheque (2001) - A Night of Tragedy in Tel Aviv

The year 2001 was marked by a series of horrifying suicide bombings, and one of the most devastating incidents during this tumultuous period was the attack on the Dolphinarium discotheque in Tel Aviv. This chapter delves into the planning, strategies, consequences, and impact of the suicide bombing that took the lives of 21 people, most of whom were teenagers, and left dozens more injured. Hamas claimed responsibility for this act of terror.

The Prelude: Planning and Strategy

The attack on the Dolphinarium discotheque was not an isolated event but part of a broader strategy employed by Hamas, the Islamic Resistance Movement. This strategy involved suicide bombings, carefully planned and executed to maximize casualties and psychological impact, instill fear, and amplify the organization's message of resistance.

In the case of the Dolphinarium bombing, the attackers, motivated by their extremist beliefs, carefully selected the target - a popular gathering place for young people. The choice of this venue during the summer season was deliberate, as it was sure to be filled with teenagers enjoying their evening.

A Night of Horror

On June 1, 2001, a suicide bomber entered the vicinity of the Dolphinarium discotheque in Tel Aviv. As the night wore on, young people danced and celebrated life within the vibrant atmosphere of the nightclub. Unbeknownst to them, a deadly threat was lurking.

At the stroke of midnight, when the discotheque was at its liveliest, the suicide bomber detonated his explosive device. The blast tore through the heart of the crowd, causing immediate chaos, devastation, and heart-wrenching scenes of panic and suffering.

Casualties and Impact

The consequences of the Dolphinarium bombing were devastating. Twenty-one people lost their lives that night, the majority of them teenagers, and dozens of others suffered injuries, some of which were life-altering. Families were shattered, and a pall of grief descended over Tel Aviv.

The attack had a profound impact not only on the victims and their loved ones but also on the entire nation of Israel. It was a stark reminder of the relentless cycle of violence that had plagued the region for decades.

Hamas's Claim of Responsibility

Hamas, the organization behind this act of terror, did not hesitate to claim responsibility for the Dolphinarium bombing. For its leaders, suicide bombings were perceived as legitimate means of resistance in the context of the conflict. They believed that such acts could draw international attention to the Palestinian cause and put pressure on the Israeli government.

International Response and Designation as a Terrorist Organization

The international community reacted with shock and condemnation to the attack on the Dolphinarium discotheque. Deliberate targeting of civilians, particularly teenagers, was viewed as a grave breach of humanitarian and international laws.

Hamas's involvement in acts of terror, such as the Dolphinarium bombing, led to its designation as a terrorist organization by numerous countries and entities. This status further entrenched its international isolation.

The Dolphinarium discotheque bombing remains a haunting memory, a testament to the enduring tragedy of the Israeli-Palestinian conflict. It serves as a poignant reminder of the urgent need for a peaceful resolution and an end to the cycle of violence that has caused immeasurable suffering to both Israeli and Palestinian communities.

(iii). Passover Massacre (2002) - A Tragedy During a Time of Celebration

In March 2002, a horrifying act of violence disrupted the celebration of Passover, one of the most significant holidays in the Jewish calendar. A suicide bomber targeted a Passover Seder in a hotel in Netanya, Israel, resulting in the loss of 30 lives and numerous injuries. Once again, Hamas claimed responsibility for this heinous act.

The Prelude: Planning and Strategy

The Passover Massacre was not an isolated incident but part of a broader strategy employed by Hamas, the Islamic Resistance Movement. Suicide bombings were a preferred tactic in their arsenal, used to sow fear, inflict significant casualties, and amplify their message of resistance.

In the case of the Passover Massacre, meticulous planning went into the operation. The target - a Passover Seder, a festive and symbolic occasion that brings families together - was chosen deliberately. The intent was to shatter the joyous atmosphere and create a lasting impact.

A Night of Celebration Turned Tragedy

The Passover Seder, a time for families to come together, recount their history, and celebrate their freedom, turned into a night of unimaginable horror on March 27, 2002. Families and friends gathered at the Park Hotel in Netanya to observe this sacred tradition.

As participants began the Seder meal, a suicide bomber entered the hotel. At a moment when unity, hope, and the promise of freedom were being celebrated, the attacker detonated the explosive device. The resulting explosion was a brutal interruption, shattering the festive atmosphere and causing immediate chaos and suffering.

Casualties and Impact

The consequences of the Passover Massacre were heart-wrenching. Thirty individuals lost their lives, and numerous others suffered injuries, both physical and psychological. Families were left in mourning, forever scarred by the tragedy.

The attack was not limited to the immediate victims and their loved ones. It reverberated throughout the nation of Israel, casting a shadow over the entire Passover holiday and the collective consciousness of the Jewish people.

Hamas's Claim of Responsibility

Hamas claimed responsibility for the Passover Massacre, as it had for previous acts of terror. Suicide bombings were seen as a legitimate means of resistance in the eyes of the organization's leaders. They believed that such acts could draw international attention to the Palestinian cause and pressure the Israeli government.

International Response and Designation as a Terrorist Organization

The international community reacted with outrage to the Passover Massacre. Deliberate targeting of civilians during a religious celebration was viewed as a flagrant violation of humanitarian and international laws.

The involvement of Hamas in acts of terror, such as the Passover Massacre, contributed to its designation as a terrorist organization by numerous countries and entities. The international community stood firm in condemning such actions and calling for an end to the cycle of violence in the Israeli-Palestinian conflict.

The Passover Massacre serves as a somber reminder of the human toll exacted by the ongoing conflict and the urgent need for a peaceful resolution. It is a testament to the profound impact of violence on both Israeli and Palestinian communities and the shared responsibility of the international community to work towards a lasting solution.

(iv). Kiryat HaYovel Supermarket Bombing (2002) - A Grim Day in Jerusalem

In March 2002, a suicide bomber struck a supermarket in Jerusalem's Kiryat HaYovel neighborhood, further adding to the tragic toll of violence during the Israeli-Palestinian conflict. This chapter delves into the planning, strategies, consequences, and impact of the Kiryat HaYovel supermarket bombing, an attack that killed two people and wounded dozens. As in previous instances, Hamas claimed responsibility for this act.

The Prelude: Planning and Strategy

The Kiryat HaYovel supermarket bombing was part of a broader strategy employed by Hamas, the Islamic Resistance Movement. Suicide bombings were a preferred tactic in their arsenal, used to instill fear, inflict casualties, and further their message of resistance.

In planning this attack, the choice of target - a supermarket in a residential neighborhood - was deliberate. The aim was to strike at the heart of daily life, targeting civilians going about their daily routines.

A Day of Dread

On a day that started like any other in Kiryat HaYovel, March 29, 2002, a suicide bomber entered a local supermarket. Shoppers went about their business, unaware of the impending tragedy.

At an opportune moment, the attacker detonated the explosive device. The resulting explosion was a devastating interruption of the peaceful setting. Panic and chaos erupted, and the consequences were immediate and severe.

Casualties and Impact

The consequences of the Kiryat HaYovel supermarket bombing were heartrending. Two people lost their lives, and dozens were wounded, some of them severely. Families were left to grapple with grief and injuries sustained during what should have been an ordinary day.

This attack, like others, had repercussions that extended far beyond the immediate victims and their loved ones. It underscored the persistent threat of violence that hung over Jerusalem and the broader Israeli-Palestinian conflict.

Hamas's Claim of Responsibility

Hamas was quick to claim responsibility for the Kiryat HaYovel bombing, as it had for previous acts of terror. The organization's leaders considered such acts as legitimate means of resistance in the context of the conflict, aimed at drawing international attention to the Palestinian cause and pressuring the Israeli government.

International Response and Designation as a Terrorist Organization

The international community responded with condemnation to the Kiryat HaYovel bombing. Deliberate attacks on civilian targets were viewed as a breach of humanitarian and international laws. Hamas's involvement in such acts contributed to its designation as a terrorist organization by numerous countries and entities.

The Kiryat HaYovel supermarket bombing serves as yet another poignant example of the human cost of the Israeli-Palestinian conflict. It underscores the need for a peaceful resolution and the responsibility of the international community to work toward a lasting solution to the ongoing violence in the region.

(v) Egged Bus 32A (2002) - A City Shaken by Terror

In March 2002, the city of Haifa experienced a horrific act of terror that left its residents in shock and mourning. A suicide bomber targeted an Egged bus, resulting in the loss of 17 lives and injuries to over 40 people. As with previous attacks, Hamas claimed responsibility for this act of violence.

The Prelude: Planning and Strategy

The bombing of Egged Bus 32A was part of Hamas's overarching strategy to employ suicide bombings as a means of resistance against Israeli forces. These attacks were carefully orchestrated to create fear, cause casualties, and amplify the organization's message of defiance.

In planning this attack, the choice of target - a public bus - was no accident. Buses were symbolic of everyday life, and targeting them aimed to instill terror in the hearts of civilians.

A Day of Horror in Haifa

On a fateful day in March 2002, residents of Haifa boarded Egged Bus 32A, expecting a routine commute. The suicide bomber, concealed among the passengers, bided their time.

At a moment when the bus was filled with commuters and families, the attacker detonated the explosive device. The blast tore through the vehicle, causing chaos, devastation, and an immediate need for rescue and medical assistance.

Casualties and Impact

The consequences of the Egged Bus 32A bombing were profound and heart-wrenching. Seventeen people lost their lives, and over 40 others were injured, some with life-changing wounds. Families were left to grapple with grief, and the scars of that day would be felt for years to come.

This attack, like previous ones, sent shockwaves through the city and beyond. It was a stark reminder of the constant threat of violence that hung over the region.

Hamas's Claim of Responsibility

Hamas claimed responsibility for the Egged Bus 32A bombing, as it had for previous acts of terror. The organization's leaders viewed suicide bombings as a legitimate means of resistance in the context of the conflict, with the intent of drawing international attention to the Palestinian cause and exerting pressure on the Israeli government.

International Response and Designation as a Terrorist Organization

The international community responded with condemnation to the Egged Bus 32A bombing. Deliberate attacks on civilian targets were widely regarded as a violation of humanitarian and international laws. Hamas's involvement in such acts contributed to its designation as a terrorist organization by numerous countries and entities.

The Egged Bus 32A bombing serves as yet another somber example of the human toll exacted by the Israeli-Palestinian conflict. It underscores the urgent need for a peaceful resolution and the shared responsibility of the international community to work towards ending the cycle of violence in the region.

2.2. Rocket Attacks:

(i) Gaza War (2008-2009) - Operation Cast Lead:

The Gaza War of 2008-2009, known as Operation Cast Lead, was a critical juncture in the ongoing Israeli-Palestinian conflict. During this conflict, Hamas unleashed a significant barrage of rockets from the Gaza Strip into southern Israel. This chapter delves into the planning, strategies, support, casualties, and impact of the Gaza War, which resulted in a devastating wave of rocket attacks by Hamas.

The Prelude: Planning and Strategy

Operation Cast Lead was a culmination of mounting tensions in the region. In the lead-up to the conflict, Hamas had been gradually increasing its rocket attacks on Israeli towns and cities near the Gaza Strip. The Israeli government viewed this as an intolerable threat to its civilian population.

The planning and strategy behind Operation Cast Lead were complex. Hamas aimed to challenge Israeli security measures and provoke a response. Their strategy included launching rockets with longer ranges, putting a broader swath of Israeli territory within reach. Israel's strategy, in turn, was to halt the rocket fire through a large-scale military operation in Gaza.

The Rocket Attacks

During Operation Cast Lead, Hamas fired a substantial number of rockets into southern Israel, targeting towns like Sderot and Ashkelon. These rocket attacks were relentless, causing fear and chaos among Israeli civilians. The range of the rockets meant that more substantial populations were under threat, leading to casualties and extensive property damage.

Impact on Israeli Civilians

The impact on Israeli civilians was profound. They were forced to live under constant threat, with rocket sirens becoming a routine part of daily life. Residents of the southern towns bore the brunt of the attacks, facing physical and psychological trauma. Schools and businesses were disrupted, and normal life came to a standstill.

Israeli Response and Casualties

In response to the rocket attacks, Israel launched a large-scale military operation in Gaza. This operation, involving airstrikes and a ground incursion, sought to weaken Hamas's capabilities and halt the rocket fire.

The casualties on both sides were significant. Palestinian casualties, including civilians, were high, and the widespread destruction in Gaza drew international attention and condemnation. On the Israeli side, while there were fewer casualties, the impact on civilian life and infrastructure was substantial.

International Response

The international community responded with a mixture of support and criticism. Israel's actions drew condemnation for the loss of civilian life and destruction in Gaza, while its right to defend itself from rocket attacks was also recognized by many countries.

The Gaza War of 2008-2009 exemplified the devastating impact of rocket attacks and military operations on both Israeli and Palestinian civilians. It underscored the complex challenges in finding a peaceful resolution to the Israeli-Palestinian conflict, a goal that remains elusive to this day.

(ii) Operation Pillar of Defense (2012) - A Barrage of Rockets and Eight Days of Conflict

In November 2012, the Israeli-Palestinian conflict entered a new and turbulent phase with Operation Pillar of Defense. This operation, initiated when an Israeli airstrike targeted Ahmed Jabari, a senior Hamas military leader, set the stage for a significant wave of rocket attacks from Gaza into southern Israel. This chapter delves into the planning, strategies, support, casualties, and impact of this eight-day conflict that shook both Israel and Gaza.

The Prelude: Planning and Strategy

Operation Pillar of Defense was not a sudden eruption of hostilities but a response to escalating tensions in the region. The Israeli government had been growing increasingly concerned about the continuous rocket attacks launched by Hamas and other militant groups in Gaza. The situation reached a breaking point with the targeted airstrike on Ahmed Jabari, a prominent figure within Hamas.

Hamas's planning and strategy for Operation Pillar of Defense were two-fold. First, they sought to draw international attention to the Palestinian cause by provoking an Israeli response. Second, they aimed to challenge Israeli security measures by firing rockets with longer ranges, putting more significant Israeli population centers within reach. Israel, in turn, planned a military campaign to halt the rocket fire.

Rocket Attacks and Their Impact

The rocket attacks during Operation Pillar of Defense were extensive and relentless. Rockets were fired from Gaza into southern Israel, reaching cities like Beersheba, Ashdod, and Tel Aviv. The attacks created a climate of fear and insecurity among Israeli civilians, who were forced to take shelter and live with the constant threat of incoming rockets.

Impact on Israeli Civilians

The impact on Israeli civilians was severe. Daily life was disrupted, schools were closed, businesses were affected, and many people were left traumatized by the experience. Casualties and injuries among Israeli civilians were reported, although the Iron Dome missile defense system intercepted many of the incoming rockets, mitigating the potential harm.

Israeli Response and Casualties

In response to the rocket attacks, Israel launched Operation Pillar of Defense, a military campaign that combined airstrikes with a ground incursion into Gaza. The aim was to weaken Hamas's military capabilities and halt the rocket fire.

The conflict resulted in casualties on both sides. In Gaza, there were Palestinian casualties, including civilians, and widespread destruction. On the Israeli side, while there were fewer casualties, the impact on civilian life and infrastructure was substantial.

International Response

The international response to Operation Pillar of Defense was mixed. Israel's actions were criticized for causing civilian casualties and infrastructure damage in Gaza. Simultaneously, many countries recognized Israel's right to defend itself from rocket attacks, underlining the complexities of the Israeli-Palestinian conflict.

Operation Pillar of Defense, with its wave of rocket attacks and military response, added another layer of complexity to the ongoing conflict. It showcased the challenges of finding a peaceful resolution and the enduring impact of violence on both Israeli and Palestinian communities.

(iii) Operation Protective Edge (2014) - A 50-Day Conflict of Rockets and Response

In the summer of 2014, the Israeli-Palestinian conflict escalated dramatically with Operation Protective Edge. Hamas fired thousands of rockets into Israel, triggering a formidable Israeli response that included airstrikes and a ground incursion into Gaza. This chapter delves into the planning, strategies, support, casualties, and the international response to this 50-day conflict that left a lasting impact on both sides.

The Prelude: Planning and Strategy

Operation Protective Edge was the culmination of rising tensions between Israel and Hamas. The situation had been deteriorating for months, with an increasing number of rocket attacks launched by Hamas from the Gaza Strip. The abduction and murder of three Israeli teenagers in June 2014 further exacerbated the situation.

Hamas's strategy was multi-faceted. The organization aimed to challenge Israeli security measures by firing rockets at population centers across southern Israel. Their rockets had increased range and destructive power, allowing them to reach further into Israeli territory. At the same time, they sought to draw international attention to their cause by provoking a substantial Israeli response.

Israel's strategy for Operation Protective Edge included a combination of airstrikes and a ground incursion into Gaza. The primary goal was to degrade Hamas's military capabilities and put a stop to the rocket fire that threatened the safety of Israeli civilians.

Rocket Attacks and Their Impact

Hamas launched thousands of rockets into Israel during the course of Operation Protective Edge. The rockets reached cities and towns in southern Israel, including Ashdod,

Ashkelon, Beersheba, and even Tel Aviv. This extensive rocket fire created panic and fear among Israeli civilians, forcing them to seek shelter and live under the constant threat of incoming rockets.

Impact on Israeli Civilians

The impact on Israeli civilians was profound. Daily life came to a standstill, with schools and businesses disrupted, and many individuals and families traumatized by the ongoing attacks. The Iron Dome missile defense system intercepted many rockets, but some still managed to cause casualties and damage.

Israeli Response and Casualties

In response to the rocket attacks, Israel launched Operation Protective Edge, a comprehensive military campaign. Israeli forces conducted airstrikes to target Hamas positions and infrastructure in Gaza, and a ground incursion aimed to degrade Hamas's capabilities.

The conflict resulted in casualties on both sides. In Gaza, Palestinian casualties, including civilians, were significant, and there was extensive damage to infrastructure. On the Israeli side, although there were fewer casualties, the impact on civilian life and infrastructure was substantial.

International Response

The international response to Operation Protective Edge was substantial. Many countries and international organizations expressed deep concern over the civilian casualties and destruction in Gaza. Simultaneously, they recognized Israel's right to defend itself from rocket attacks.

Operation Protective Edge left a lasting impact on the Israeli-Palestinian conflict, underscoring the complexities of finding a peaceful resolution and the enduring consequences of violence on both Israeli and Palestinian communities.

(iv) Operation Protective Edge (2018) - Renewed Rocket Fire and Escalation

In July 2018, the Israeli-Palestinian conflict experienced another episode of heightened tensions and violence with the resurgence of rocket attacks. This time, Hamas and other militant groups in Gaza fired rockets into southern Israel, eliciting a significant Israeli response. This chapter explores the planning, strategies, support, casualties, and impact of this exchange of rocket fire that once again plunged the region into turmoil.

The Prelude: Planning and Strategy

Operation Protective Edge in 2018 was not an isolated event but part of a recurring cycle of tensions. The situation had been deteriorating with sporadic rocket attacks launched by Hamas and other groups in Gaza. These attacks were an ongoing source of concern for Israel, leading to an increasingly tense environment.

Hamas's strategy, similar to previous conflicts, involved firing rockets into southern Israel to challenge its security measures and provoke a substantial Israeli response. The rocket attacks were intended to target Israeli towns and cities, posing a direct threat to civilian populations.

Rocket Attacks and Their Impact

The rocket attacks during Operation Protective Edge in 2018 were extensive. Rockets were launched from Gaza, reaching towns and cities in southern Israel. These attacks once again created fear and uncertainty among Israeli civilians, who were forced to seek shelter and grapple with the constant threat of incoming rockets.

Impact on Israeli Civilians

The impact on Israeli civilians was significant. Daily life was disrupted, schools and businesses were affected, and residents of southern Israeli towns lived under the constant threat of rocket fire. The Iron Dome missile defense system intercepted many of the rockets, but some managed to cause casualties and damage.

Israeli Response and Casualties

In response to the rocket attacks, Israel carried out airstrikes to target Hamas positions and infrastructure in Gaza. These airstrikes were part of an effort to degrade the military capabilities of the militant groups responsible for the rocket fire.

The conflict resulted in casualties on both sides. In Gaza, there were Palestinian casualties, including civilians, and damage to infrastructure. On the Israeli side, although there were fewer casualties, the impact on civilian life and infrastructure was substantial.

International Response

The international response to Operation Protective Edge in 2018 mirrored previous conflicts. Many countries and international organizations expressed concern over the civilian casualties and destruction in Gaza while recognizing Israel's right to defend itself from rocket attacks.

Operation Protective Edge in 2018 served as a stark reminder of the ongoing challenges in finding a peaceful resolution to the Israeli-Palestinian conflict. It highlighted the enduring impact of violence on both Israeli and Palestinian communities, underscoring the complexities of the situation in the region.

(v) May 2021 Conflict - A Renewed Wave of Rockets and Israeli Response

In May 2021, the Israeli-Palestinian conflict flared up once again with a significant outbreak of violence. This time, Hamas launched a large number of rockets into Israeli cities and towns, including Jerusalem and Tel Aviv. The conflict, sparked by tensions in East Jerusalem, resulted in injuries and damage to infrastructure in Israel, prompting a robust Israeli response. This chapter explores the planning, strategies, support, casualties, and impact of this recent escalation in the conflict.

The Prelude: Planning and Strategy

The May 2021 conflict was rooted in simmering tensions, particularly in East Jerusalem, where clashes had been ongoing for weeks. These tensions erupted into a full-scale confrontation when Hamas launched a barrage of rockets into Israeli cities.

Hamas's strategy involved targeting Jerusalem, Tel Aviv, and other population centers in Israel. Their rocket attacks aimed to challenge Israeli security measures and draw international attention to the Palestinian cause. The rockets used had a longer range, placing a larger portion of Israeli territory within reach.

Rocket Attacks and Their Impact

The rocket attacks during the May 2021 conflict were intense and widespread. Rockets were launched from Gaza into Israeli cities, reaching as far as Jerusalem and Tel Aviv. These attacks once again sowed fear and uncertainty among Israeli civilians, forcing them to seek shelter and grapple with the constant threat of incoming rockets.

Impact on Israeli Civilians

The impact on Israeli civilians was significant. Schools and businesses were disrupted, and residents of Israeli towns lived under the constant threat of rocket fire. The Iron Dome missile defense system intercepted many rockets, but some managed to cause casualties and damage.

Israeli Response and Casualties

In response to the rocket attacks, Israel conducted airstrikes in Gaza, targeting Hamas positions and infrastructure. The airstrikes were part of an effort to halt the rocket fire and degrade the military capabilities of the groups responsible.

The conflict resulted in casualties on both sides. In Gaza, there were Palestinian casualties, including civilians, and damage to infrastructure. On the Israeli side, although there were fewer casualties, the impact on civilian life and infrastructure was substantial.

International Response

The international response to the May 2021 conflict was substantial. Many countries and international organizations expressed deep concern over the civilian casualties and destruction in Gaza. Simultaneously, they recognized Israel's right to defend itself from rocket attacks.

The May 2021 conflict served as a reminder of the enduring challenges in finding a peaceful resolution to the Israeli-Palestinian conflict. It underscored the complexities of the situation and the lasting impact of violence on both Israeli and Palestinian communities.

2.3.   Tunnels - The Underground Arsenal of Hamas

In addition to rocket attacks and suicide bombings, Hamas has employed a network of tunnels as a distinctive element of its military strategy. These tunnels, some of which extended into Israeli territory, served various purposes, including smuggling weapons and launching attacks against Israeli soldiers and civilians. This chapter explores the planning, strategies, consequences, and impact of Hamas's tunnel network.

The Prelude: Planning and Strategy

Hamas's tunnel network was not a haphazard creation but a calculated part of its military planning. These underground passages were designed to serve multiple functions. While some tunnels were used for smuggling, others were created to infiltrate Israeli territory and carry out attacks on soldiers and civilians.

Hamas's strategic approach to tunnel construction was systematic, reflecting an understanding that these subterranean pathways offered a distinct advantage. They allowed the movement of fighters and weapons while concealing these activities from Israeli surveillance.

A Hidden Arsenal Beneath the Surface

The presence of these tunnels beneath the surface went largely unnoticed by those on both sides of the Israeli-Gaza border. Hamas's ingenuity in tunnel construction was evident in the network's extent, intricacy, and ability to go undetected. Tunnels were constructed with multiple access points, often hidden beneath homes, mosques, and other civilian structures.

Hamas operatives used these tunnels for smuggling arms and munitions, such as rockets, into the Gaza Strip. This underground infrastructure provided a secure conduit for maintaining the organization's military capabilities.

Causalities and Impact

Hamas's tunnel network had significant consequences. Israeli forces discovered and destroyed many of these tunnels, often leading to clashes with Hamas operatives. In some instances, the tunnels were used for surprise attacks on Israeli soldiers and civilians near the border.

The existence of these tunnels created a climate of fear and insecurity among Israeli communities in the vicinity of the Gaza Strip. Residents lived with the knowledge that underground threats could emerge at any moment.

Hamas's Claim of Responsibility

Hamas has openly acknowledged the existence of its tunnel network. While the organization has defended its use of tunnels as a means of resistance against Israeli forces, it has been widely criticized for placing military infrastructure in civilian areas, which has exposed Palestinian civilians to danger.

International Response

The international community has recognized the threat posed by Hamas's tunnel network. Israel's efforts to locate and destroy these tunnels have been met with varying degrees of international support, with some countries acknowledging Israel's right to defend itself and others expressing concern over the impact on Palestinian civilians.

The tunnels have been a focal point of concern in the ongoing Israeli-Palestinian conflict, representing the complexities and risks involved in military operations in densely populated areas.

Hamas's tunnel network has been a source of conflict and concern in the region, with its existence shaping the security landscape and prompting significant responses from both sides of the Israeli-Gaza border. The tunnels are emblematic of the challenges and consequences of underground warfare in a conflict characterized by close proximity and high stakes.

2.4 Border Protest

In the vast and tumultuous tapestry of the Israeli-Palestinian conflict, these border protests lies a profound quest, one etched in the collective consciousness of Palestinians—a quest for self-determination and an end to what they perceive as the suffocating grip of Israeli occupation. Motivated by historical grievances and political aspirations, the protests are a testament to the indomitable spirit of a people yearning for justice.

The organisation which plays a key role in the strategy is Hamas-a key orchestrator in this grand performance of dissent. The border protests orchestrated by Hamas are rooted in a complex web of historical grievances, political aspirations, and the desire for international attention. At the heart of these demonstrations is the longstanding Palestinian quest for self-determination and an end to what they perceive as Israeli occupation.

While many of the border protests have been non-violent expressions of discontent, some have escalated into clashes with Israeli forces. The non-violent protests often involve marches, speeches, and symbolic acts aimed at drawing attention to the Palestinian struggle. However, in certain instances, the situation has taken a more confrontational turn, with protesters engaging in activities like stone-throwing and attempts to breach the border fence.

Hamas strategically leverages these border protests to garner international attention and condemnation of Israeli actions. The clashes serve as a rallying point for pro-Palestinian sentiments globally, sparking debates on the use of force, border security, and the broader Israeli-Palestinian conflict.

Hamas has played a central role in organizing these protests, utilizing them as a strategic tool to amplify the Palestinian cause on the global stage. The organization has mobilized its supporters, drawing on a broad base of participants, including civilians, activists, and members of various Palestinian factions.

However, the nature of the Protests remains a dilemma for many. But, the border protests waltz between the realms of non-violent expression and confrontational defiance. Peaceful marches, impassioned speeches, and symbolic acts create a poignant narrative of discontent. Yet, as the rhythm intensifies, clashes with Israeli forces disrupt the harmony. Stones thrown, fences breached—a dance that speaks of both desperation and unyielding determination.

In this charged atmosphere, Israeli forces wield their instruments of crowd control, a discordant response that reverberates globally. Tear gas mingles with the acrid scent of resistance, live ammunition punctuates the air, and casualties become the somber refrain. The Israeli response fuels the flames, creating a cacophony of conflict that echoes far beyond the border.

Hamas tends to take these protests and clashes to the next level, positions itself to amplify the impact of border protests on a global scale. These clashes become a focal point, resonating with pro-Palestinian sentiments worldwide. The international stage transforms into a platform for discussions on the ethics of force, complexities of border security, and the overarching Israeli-Palestinian drama.

As the drama unfolds, casualties mount, and humanitarian concerns come to the forefront. The protests exact a toll not only in lives lost but in the shattered remnants of a community. Women, children—the innocent casualties of a conflict that knows no boundaries. The repercussions are not just political; they are deeply human.

Therefore, the border protests orchestrated by Hamas at the Gaza-Israel border encapsulate the multifaceted nature of the Israeli-Palestinian conflict. From non-violent expressions of resistance to clashes with Israeli forces, these protests embody the deeply entrenched grievances and aspirations of the Palestinian people. As the cycle of protests and responses continues, the border remains a symbol of both resistance and the ongoing challenges in the quest for a just and lasting resolution to the conflict.

Chapter 3: Leadership and Structure

In the intricate world of Hamas, understanding its leadership and organizational structure is pivotal to comprehending its multifaceted role in the Israeli-Palestinian conflict. This chapter unveils the key figures at the helm of the organization and dissects its hierarchical structure, offering insights into how Hamas operates and makes critical decisions.

3.1 Hamas Leadership

Hamas's leadership is composed of individuals who have played instrumental roles in shaping the organization's ideology and strategies. Among the notable figures are:

1. **Sheikh Ahmed Yassin:**

Sheikh Ahmed Yassin, often regarded as the spiritual leader and co-founder of Hamas, played a pivotal role in shaping the organization's Islamist ideology and in garnering support among the Palestinian population. His influence extended beyond the leadership position he held within Hamas, as he provided spiritual guidance and a charismatic voice to the organization. Sheikh Yassin's commitment to Hamas's Islamist ideology, which framed the struggle against Israeli occupation as a religious duty, resonated with many Palestinians seeking a more faith-centered approach to the conflict. His role in the early formation of Hamas and his continued leadership throughout its history significantly impacted the organization's development and strategies. Sheikh Yassin's journey was a testament to his unwavering commitment to Hamas's Islamist ideology and the Palestinian cause.

Born in 1937 in what is now the Gaza Strip, Sheikh Yassin's early life was marked by a deep connection to his faith and the Palestinian struggle. As a young man, he became involved in various Islamic organizations, but it was in 1973 that he, along with a group of like-minded individuals, laid the foundation for what would become Hamas.

Sheikh Yassin's spiritual guidance was instrumental in shaping Hamas's Islamist ideology. His charismatic leadership and fiery sermons resonated with a segment of the Palestinian population seeking a more religiously grounded approach to the conflict. His message intertwined faith with resistance, framing the struggle against Israeli occupation as a religious duty.

Sheikh Yassin's leadership helped garner support for Hamas, particularly in the Gaza Strip. Under his guidance, the organization not only drew ideological strength from its

Islamic roots but also gained a following among Palestinians disillusioned by the secular approach of other factions.

Sheikh Yassin's leadership was not without controversy, especially due to his unwavering stance against the State of Israel. His charisma and influence extended to the political and militant wings of Hamas, where his vision continued to shape the organization's strategies and actions.

The assassination of Sheikh Ahmed Yassin in an Israeli airstrike in 2004 marked a significant turning point in Hamas's history. While his physical presence was lost, his legacy and the Islamist ideology he championed continued to guide the organization's path.

Sheikh Ahmed Yassin, made significant contributions to the organization and the Palestinian cause. Some of his notable achievements and influences include:

i. **Founding of Hamas**: Sheikh Ahmed Yassin played a pivotal role in the founding of Hamas in 1987 during the First Intifada. This marked the establishment of a Palestinian organization with a clear Islamic and militant focus.

ii. **Inspiring Palestinian Resistance**: Yassin's leadership and teachings provided inspiration to a new generation of Palestinians, motivating them to resist Israeli occupation. He was a symbol of resilience and steadfastness in the face of adversity.

iii. **Mobilizing Grassroots Support**: Yassin's charismatic leadership and religious authority helped mobilize grassroots support for Hamas. He had the ability to connect with and rally Palestinians from various walks of life behind the organization's cause.

iv. **Advocating for Armed Resistance**: Yassin's unwavering advocacy for armed resistance against Israeli forces became a cornerstone of Hamas's ideology. His influence was instrumental in shaping the organization's commitment to military struggle.

v. **Expanding Hamas's Influence:** Under Yassin's leadership, Hamas expanded its influence beyond the Gaza Strip and into the West Bank. This expansion allowed the organization to become a prominent player in Palestinian politics.

vi. **Symbol of Palestinian Resistance:** Sheikh Ahmed Yassin became a symbol of Palestinian resistance against Israeli occupation. His prominence on the global stage drew attention to the Palestinian struggle for self-determination.

vii. **Humanitarian and Social Services**: Yassin and Hamas were involved in providing social services and humanitarian assistance to Palestinians in need. This included running schools, hospitals, and welfare programs, which created a social safety net for many in the community.

viii. **Prison Release**: Yassin's capture and imprisonment by Israel in the 1980s and his subsequent release in a prisoner exchange in 1997 further elevated his status as a symbol of Palestinian resistance.

Sheikh Ahmed Yassin's achievements primarily revolved around his founding role within Hamas, his leadership in promoting Palestinian resistance, and his ability to inspire and mobilize Palestinians in their quest for self-determination. His legacy continues to have a profound impact on the Palestinian territories and the broader Israeli-Palestinian conflict.

2. Khaled Mashal: Navigating Diplomacy on the Global Stage

Within the intricate tapestry of Hamas's leadership, Khaled Mashal stands out as a prominent figure in the organization's political bureau. His role in representing Hamas on the international stage has been instrumental in shaping the organization's diplomatic engagement and navigating the complex terrain of the Israeli-Palestinian conflict.

Khaled Mashal's journey as a key Hamas leader began in the heart of the Palestinian territories, and it has since extended to the global arena. Born in the West Bank in 1956, he became politically active during his years as a student at Kuwait University. It was during this time that he joined the ranks of the Palestinian diaspora and embraced the cause of the Palestinian people.

Mashal's rise within Hamas was marked by his leadership skills, strategic acumen, and ability to engage with international actors. His political career within the organization led him to represent Hamas in various diplomatic negotiations and engagements. His role was crucial in projecting Hamas's stance and interests to the world, particularly when it came to negotiating with other nations and international bodies.

Mashal's tenure as the leader of Hamas's political bureau, which began in 1996, coincided with a period of significant diplomatic challenges. He was at the helm when Hamas decisively won the Palestinian legislative elections in 2006, a victory that led to his leadership taking on even greater international significance.

Under Mashal's guidance, Hamas navigated complex diplomatic landscapes, engaging in discussions and negotiations aimed at addressing the longstanding Israeli-Palestinian conflict. These efforts were often met with mixed reactions, reflecting the divisive nature of the conflict and differing perspectives on Hamas's legitimacy.

While some nations and international bodies considered Hamas a terrorist organization and refused to engage with it, others saw it as a legitimate political entity representing the Palestinian people's interests. Mashal's leadership in these circumstances underscored the challenges and complexities involved in advocating for Hamas on the global stage.

Khaled Mashal, a prominent figure within Hamas, has had a significant impact on the organization's political and diplomatic activities. Some of his notable achievements and contributions include:

i. **International Representation:** Khaled Mashal has been a key representative of Hamas on the international stage. His diplomatic engagement and advocacy have aimed to increase global awareness of the Palestinian cause and garner support for the organization.

ii. **Negotiations and Truces**: Mashal has played a role in negotiations and truce agreements with Israel. His involvement in ceasefire efforts reflects a commitment to finding peaceful solutions to the Israeli-Palestinian conflict and alleviating the suffering of Palestinian civilians.

iii. **Brokering Prisoner Exchange**: Mashal was involved in negotiations that led to significant prisoner exchanges between Hamas and Israel. Notable exchanges, such as the one that secured the release of Israeli soldier Gilad Shalit, showcased his ability to broker complex deals.

iv. **Managing Hamas's International Relations**: Mashal has navigated relations with regional actors, such as Iran, Qatar, and Turkey, securing political and financial support for Hamas. These relationships have contributed to the organization's sustainability.

v. **Political Bureau Leadership**: As a member of the Hamas Political Bureau, Mashal has provided strategic direction and leadership to the organization's political activities. This role has been instrumental in shaping Hamas's political strategies and policies.

vi. **Public Advocacy:** Mashal has been a vocal advocate for the Palestinian cause, using his position to address international audiences and draw attention to the plight of Palestinians in the occupied territories.

Khaled Mashal's achievements lie in his leadership on the international stage and his diplomatic efforts to advance the Palestinian cause. His ability to navigate complex regional and international relations has been crucial in maintaining Hamas's visibility and relevance in the Israeli-Palestinian conflict.

3. Ismail Haniyeh: Bridging Political Leadership

In the labyrinthine world of Hamas, Ismail Haniyeh emerges as a key leader who has played a significant role in the organization's political and administrative landscape. His journey from the Prime Minister of the Palestinian Authority to becoming the head of Hamas's political bureau is emblematic of the intricate political dynamics within the organization.

Ismail Haniyeh was born in the Shati refugee camp in the Gaza Strip in 1963. His early years were marked by a commitment to education and a burgeoning engagement in Palestinian political activities. This led him to join the ranks of the Palestinian Islamist movement and, subsequently, to become a prominent figure within Hamas.

Haniyeh's leadership trajectory within Hamas took a significant turn when he assumed the role of the Prime Minister of the Palestinian Authority in 2006. This appointment came after Hamas decisively won the Palestinian legislative elections, a victory that marked a turning point in Palestinian politics.

During his tenure as Prime Minister, Ismail Haniyeh was at the helm of the Palestinian Authority, which governed the West Bank and the Gaza Strip. His leadership faced complex challenges, including international isolation and financial constraints, as Western nations cut aid to the Palestinian Authority due to Hamas's victory and refusal to recognize Israel.

Haniyeh's ability to navigate this complex landscape was instrumental. He played a central role in shaping the policies and strategies of Hamas and was a key interlocutor in the faction's dealings with various international actors. His leadership contributed to Hamas's resilience and ability to maintain its presence and governance in the Gaza Strip.

In the subsequent years, Ismail Haniyeh continued to rise within Hamas's ranks and, in 2017, he assumed the position of the head of the organization's political bureau. In this role, he oversees the organization's political and diplomatic activities, representing Hamas in the international arena.

Haniyeh's leadership has been marked by challenges, successes, and adaptability, making him a pivotal figure in the political leadership of Hamas. As we delve deeper into the labyrinthine world of the organization, his journey and contributions provide invaluable insights into its intricate dynamics.

Ismail Haniyeh has had a significant political career within Hamas and the Palestinian territories. Some of his notable achievements and contributions include:

i. **Leadership within Hamas:** Haniyeh has been a prominent leader within Hamas, rising through the organization's ranks and assuming pivotal roles in both its political and administrative structures.

ii. **Prime Minister of the Palestinian Authority:** From 2006 to 2014, Haniyeh served as the Prime Minister of the

Palestinian Authority. This was a period marked by complex political dynamics, including the challenges of governing in the West Bank and Gaza Strip.

iii. **Balancing Act**: Haniyeh's leadership has often required a delicate balancing act between the principles of Hamas and the political realities of governing in the Palestinian territories. His ability to navigate these complexities has been a significant achievement.

iv. **Representing Hamas Internationally:** As the head of Hamas's political bureau, Haniyeh represents the organization in international forums. This role has involved engaging with regional and international actors to garner support for the Palestinian cause.

v. **Diplomatic Engagement**: Haniyeh has been involved in diplomatic efforts to secure long-term ceasefires and truces with Israel. His involvement in negotiations and dialogue reflects his commitment to finding peaceful solutions to the Israeli-Palestinian conflict.

vi. **Navigating Regional Relations:** Haniyeh has played a role in strengthening ties with countries such as Qatar and Turkey, which have provided political and financial support to Hamas. These efforts have been crucial for the organization's sustainability.

Haniyeh's achievements lie in his adaptability and pragmatism in dealing with the multifaceted challenges of the Israeli-Palestinian conflict. While his leadership has not been without controversy, it has allowed Hamas to maintain its political relevance and engage with the international community.

4. Yahya Sinwar: Guiding the Gaza Strip

Within the intricate fabric of Hamas, Yahya Sinwar emerges as a central figure, wielding substantial influence over the organization's activities and policies in the Gaza Strip. His journey through the ranks of Hamas and his current leadership role provide a critical perspective on the organization's activities in this region.

Yahya Sinwar was born in Khan Yunis in the southern Gaza Strip in 1962. His early years were marked by engagement in Palestinian resistance activities, and he became involved with the Palestinian Islamist movement, eventually leading to his affiliation with Hamas. Sinwar's dedication to the Palestinian cause and his commitment to the organization's goals quickly propelled him into leadership positions.

Sinwar's journey within Hamas's leadership has been marked by significant phases. He was imprisoned by Israel for over two decades, during which he continued to play a role within Hamas's imprisoned leadership. His steadfast commitment to the organization and its goals further solidified his position as a key figure in the movement.

Upon his release in 2011 as part of a prisoner exchange, Sinwar's influence and leadership within Hamas expanded. He played a pivotal role in Hamas's political and military activities and was involved in negotiations to secure the release of Palestinian prisoners.

In 2017, Yahya Sinwar ascended to the position of the leader of Hamas in the Gaza Strip. His leadership has been instrumental in shaping the organization's strategies and activities within this region. Under his guidance, Hamas has continued its governance in the Gaza Strip, which has faced complex challenges, including isolation and economic constraints.

Yahya Sinwar's leadership of Hamas in the Gaza Strip has been marked by several key factors and contributions that have significantly progressed the organization's activities and policies in the region.

i. **Militant Leadership:** Under Yahya Sinwar's leadership, the Gaza Strip has seen an increase in militant activities. This includes not only rocket attacks into Israeli territory but also efforts to develop and enhance military capabilities. Sinwar has been a proponent of building up Hamas's military infrastructure, which has had a direct impact on the group's ability to engage with Israeli forces.

ii. **Consolidation of Power:** Sinwar's leadership has seen the further consolidation of power within the Gaza Strip. This has included exerting control over various aspects of governance, security, and civil administration. His leadership style has been marked by a pragmatic and often forceful approach in maintaining authority.

iii. **Regional and International Relations:** Sinwar's leadership has also seen attempts to navigate relations with regional and international actors. This includes efforts to secure political and financial support from countries such as Qatar, as well as negotiations with international mediators to establish a long-term ceasefire with Israel.

iv. **Social and Humanitarian Initiatives:** While known for his militant stance, Sinwar has also been involved in various social and humanitarian initiatives within the Gaza Strip. These efforts have included addressing issues such as healthcare, education, and infrastructure development, aiming to improve the lives of the Palestinian population in the region.

As we explore the multifaceted nature of Hamas and its impact on the Gaza Strip, Yahya Sinwar's leadership provides a critical lens through which to understand the organization's activities and policies in this complex and politically charged region. His contributions, both in terms of military strategies and governance, have significantly shaped the trajectory of Hamas in the Gaza Strip and continue to have a profound impact on the Palestinian territories.

5. Mahmoud Al-Zahar

Mahmoud Al-Zahar is a notable Palestinian political figure and a founding member of Hamas, the Islamic Resistance

Movement. His role in the organization has been instrumental in shaping the political landscape of the Palestinian territories, particularly in the Gaza Strip. Here are some key points about Mahmoud Al-Zahar:

i. **Founding Member of Hamas:** Mahmoud Al-Zahar played a foundational role in the establishment of Hamas, which emerged during the First Intifada in the late 1980s. As a co-founder, he helped shape the organization's principles, ideology, and strategies.

ii. **Political Leadership**: Al-Zahar has held various leadership positions within Hamas, including serving as the Foreign Minister of the Palestinian Authority when Hamas governed the Gaza Strip. His political leadership has been central to shaping the policies and strategies of the organization.

iii. **Strategic Decision-Making**: He has been involved in making strategic decisions for Hamas, including those related to negotiations, armed resistance, diplomacy, and international engagement. His insights and contributions have had a significant impact on the organization's direction.

iv. **Diplomatic Efforts**: Mahmoud Al-Zahar has engaged in diplomatic efforts aimed at securing ceasefires and truces in the Israeli-Palestinian conflict. His involvement in negotiations and dialogue reflects a commitment to finding peaceful solutions to the ongoing conflict.

v. **Advocate for the Palestinian Cause**: He has been a prominent advocate for the Palestinian cause on the global stage. His diplomatic roles have allowed him to address international audiences, raising awareness about the challenges faced by Palestinians in the occupied territories.

vi. **Unity Initiatives**: Al-Zahar has been actively involved in initiatives aimed at achieving Palestinian unity, including reconciliation efforts between Hamas and Fatah. These endeavors seek to address internal divisions within the Palestinian leadership.

vii. **Experience and Commitment**: With a long history of involvement in Hamas and the Palestinian struggle, Mahmoud Al-Zahar brings a wealth of experience and deep commitment to the organization's goals and the broader Israeli-Palestinian conflict.

Mahmoud Al-Zahar's contributions to Hamas and the Palestinian cause have been extensive, spanning political leadership, diplomatic engagement, strategic decision-making, and advocacy. His enduring commitment to the Palestinian struggle and his role in shaping Hamas's direction have made him a respected and influential figure in Palestinian politics.

3.2 Organizational Structure

Hamas operates within a well-defined hierarchical structure that encompasses both its political and military wings. This chapter delves into the intricacies of Hamas's organizational structure, shedding light on how decisions are made and implemented within the organization. Understanding this structure is pivotal to comprehending how Hamas operates and navigates the complex landscape of the Israeli-Palestinian conflict.

The Political Bureau: Shaping Diplomacy and Strategy

At the helm of Hamas's political leadership is the Political Bureau, which is often headed by influential figures such as

Khaled Mashal. This segment of the organization is responsible for shaping Hamas's diplomatic and strategic approaches. It plays a crucial role in international relations and negotiations, representing Hamas on the global stage.

The Political Bureau is tasked with making decisions related to diplomatic initiatives, ceasefires, negotiations, and other key political aspects of Hamas's engagement in the Israeli-Palestinian conflict. Its members interact with foreign governments, international organizations, and other Palestinian factions to advance the organization's goals and interests. The Political Bureau's decisions can have far-reaching implications for the organization and the Palestinian territories as a whole.

Majlis al-Shura: The Consultative Council

Within Hamas, the Majlis al-Shura (Consultative Council) is a vital component in the decision-making process. This council consists of prominent leaders and serves as a forum for shaping the organization's policies and strategies. The Majlis al-Shura discusses and deliberates on crucial matters, making recommendations and providing guidance to the leadership.

The council role within Hamas is a crucial part of the decision-making process. It's essentially a platform where prominent leaders come together to discuss and debate important matters. The council consists of key figures within Hamas who bring their expertise and insights to the table. They deliberate on various issues, ensuring that the decisions made by Hamas align with the organization's core principles and goals.

It's interesting how this consultative approach helps Hamas maintain its ideological consistency while adapting to changing circumstances. The council's input must be invaluable for the leadership and that's absolutely needed for their mission, they operates in a complex and challenging political landscape. The consultative nature of the Majlis al-Shura provides a level of internal checks and balances that helps Hamas stay true to its mission while responding to evolving situations.

And it's not just about politics; it influences their military and social initiatives too.

The Majlis al-Shura's guidance extends to all aspects of Hamas's operations. Whether it's political decisions, military strategies, or social programs, the council's advice plays a vital role in shaping the organization's activities.

It seems like a fascinating insight into how Hamas operates internally and maintains its cohesion in the face of various challenges.

Understanding the role of the Majlis al-Shura is essential for comprehending Hamas's decision-making processes and its ability to navigate the intricate dynamics of the Israeli-Palestinian conflict.

Izz ad-Din al-Qassam Brigades: The Military Wing

Hamas's military wing, known as the Izz ad-Din al-Qassam Brigades, is responsible for armed resistance against Israeli forces and civilians. This segment of the organization operates under a military structure with various units specialized in different aspects of armed conflict. These units carry out attacks, including suicide bombings, rocket fire, and other forms of violence directed at Israeli targets.

The Izz ad-Din al-Qassam Brigades are a key component of Hamas's operations and have been at the forefront of the organization's military activities. Their actions have garnered international attention and have contributed to Hamas's classification as a terrorist organization by some countries and entities.

While the classification of Hamas as a terrorist organization is a matter of dispute, it's essential to examine the Izz ad-Din al-Qassam Brigades' role in Hamas's military operations. Their structured approach to armed resistance involves different units specializing in various aspects of conflict. This military hierarchy enables them to conduct a range of operations, from suicide bombings to rocket attacks.

Therefore, these specialized units does give them a level of tactical flexibility. However, one of the challenges that emerge from the Izz ad-Din al-Qassam Brigades' activities is the humanitarian impact on both Israeli civilians and Palestinian civilians living in proximity to the conflict zone. The use of indiscriminate tactics like rocket attacks often results in civilian casualties and property damage, which raises international concerns and garners attention, and that's a valid point. The humanitarian aspect is a critical concern. On the other hand, from a bureaucratic perspective, the Izz ad-Din al-Qassam Brigades' actions can further complicate diplomatic efforts. Their involvement in violent acts makes it difficult to engage in peace negotiations or broker ceasefire agreements. This could be seen as a downside when seeking diplomatic solutions to the Israeli-Palestinian conflict. Because, their actions do present a significant obstacle to diplomacy. It's a complex situation where their military role has both advantages and disadvantages. Despite this, the Izz ad-Din al-Qassam Brigades remain a critical component of Hamas's military capabilities and have, in some instances, influenced the dynamics of the ongoing conflict. Balancing these aspects is essential when analyzing the broader regional situation.

Social Services: Winning Hearts and Minds

Hamas also operates an extensive network of social services, which includes providing education, healthcare, and welfare programs to the Palestinian population, particularly in the Gaza Strip. This sector of Hamas's operations serves not only as a safety net for Palestinians in need but also as a means to garner support and loyalty among the local population.

By offering these social services, Hamas seeks to address the needs of Palestinians and solidify its presence within Palestinian communities. This dual approach, combining both military and social activities, has been integral to Hamas's influence and support base.

Chapter 4: Regional and International Relations

Hamas's influence and activities extend beyond the Palestinian territories, making it a significant player in the broader regional and international context. This chapter delves into the intricate web of regional and international relations that shape Hamas's actions, policies, and standing on the global stage. Understanding these relations is essential to grasp the organization's role in the Israeli-Palestinian conflict. However, Hamas is considered a terrorist organisation by several countries and this designation poses significant challenges for Hamas on the international stage. It limits its ability to engage in diplomatic activities and access financial resources from countries that adhere to these designations. This has led Hamas to seek support from countries and organizations that do not classify it as a terrorist group.

4.1 Neighboring States and Hamas Relations

Hamas's interactions with neighboring states significantly impact its operations and the Israeli-Palestinian conflict. Two key countries in this regard are Egypt and Jordan.

4.1a Egypt

Egypt shares a border with the Gaza Strip, which has been under Hamas's control since 2007. The relationship between Hamas and Egypt has evolved over the years, with periods of tension and cooperation. Egypt has at times imposed restrictions on the movement of goods and people across the border, in part due to concerns about security and the potential for smuggling. It has also mediated ceasefire agreements between Hamas and Israel. Understanding the dynamics of the Hamas-Egypt relationship sheds light on the challenges and opportunities the organization faces.

The relationship between Egypt and Hamas is characterized by a mix of cooperation and tension. Egypt shares a border with the Gaza Strip, which has been under Hamas's control since 2007. This geographical proximity has significant implications for their relations.

Examples of this relationship include:

a. **Border Crossings**: Egypt has periodically imposed restrictions on the movement of goods and people across the border with Gaza. These restrictions are often driven by concerns about security, including the potential for weapons smuggling.

b. **Ceasefire Mediation**: Egypt has played a mediating role in brokering ceasefire agreements between Hamas and Israel. For instance, in 2014, Egypt helped negotiate a ceasefire that ended a conflict between Hamas and Israel.

c. **Humanitarian Aid**: Egypt's actions at the border have had a direct impact on the humanitarian situation in Gaza, as they affect the flow of goods, including essential supplies and aid.

d. **Bilateral Diplomacy**: Diplomatic relations between Egypt and Hamas have experienced ups and downs. Egypt's approach to Hamas has been influenced by its own political interests and regional dynamics.

e. **Regional Influence**: Egypt's involvement in negotiations and mediation efforts underlines its role as a key player in the Israeli-Palestinian conflict and the broader Middle East.

Egypt's relationship with Hamas has indeed been quite complex. It's primarily because Egypt shares a border with the Gaza Strip, which has been under Hamas's control since 2007. The geographical proximity plays a significant role in shaping their relations. Egypt has had periods of both cooperation and tension with Hamas. They've imposed restrictions on the movement of goods and people across the border at times, mainly due to security concerns and the potential for smuggling. On the other hand, Egypt has also mediated ceasefire agreements between Hamas and Israel, showing that there are opportunities for cooperation despite the challenges. This dynamic has important implications for both parties' political stability and security.

4.1b. Jordan

Jordan has historically had a complex relationship with Palestinian factions, including Hamas. The country hosts a significant Palestinian refugee population and has its own political considerations. Hamas's activities, ideologies, and regional developments have implications for Jordan's political stability and security. Examining the relationship between Hamas and Jordan provides insights into the regional dynamics and the factors influencing Jordan's foreign policy.

The relationship between Jordan and Hamas has been complex and marked by various challenges, largely due to the historical background and regional dynamics. Jordan has faced security concerns related to Hamas's activities and the potential for spillover effects from the Israeli-Palestinian conflict.

Here are some examples of the Jordan-Hamas relationship:

a. **Expulsion of Hamas Leaders**: In the late 1990s and early 2000s, Jordan expelled several Hamas leaders from the country, including Khaled Mashal, who was the head of the political bureau at the time. This move was a result of security concerns and tensions related to Hamas's activities.

b. **Security Cooperation**: Jordan has been vigilant in monitoring and countering potential security threats posed by Islamist groups, including Hamas. The government has cooperated with international efforts to combat terrorism and has worked to maintain stability in the region.

c. **Changing Dynamics**: While the relationship has been strained at times, the dynamics between Jordan and Hamas have evolved. There have been periods of relative calm and cooperation, especially in the context of broader Middle East developments.

d. **Diplomatic Considerations**: Jordan has pursued diplomatic efforts related to the Israeli-Palestinian conflict, often in coordination with the Palestinian Authority. The role it plays in these negotiations can indirectly influence its relationship with Hamas.

Jordan's relationship with Hamas is indeed quite intricate. With its significant Palestinian refugee population, the country has to navigate a complex web of political considerations and regional dynamics. Jordan has faced security concerns related to Hamas's activities, which can have a direct impact on its political stability and overall security.

On the one hand, they have to consider their Palestinian population's interests, but on the other, they must manage their relationship with neighboring Israel and maintain their own national security. And let's not forget that regional developments often influence Jordan's foreign policy decisions. The Israeli-Palestinian conflict, with Hamas being a significant player, adds another layer of complexity to the situation.

Understanding the interplay between Jordan and Hamas provides valuable insights into the broader Middle East regional dynamics and how these relationships shape foreign policies and security considerations.

4.1c. Iran: A Key Regional Ally

Iran has been a crucial regional ally for Hamas, providing financial and military support. The relationship between the two entities is rooted in common anti-Israel sentiments and shared religious ties. Iran's support has enabled Hamas to strengthen its military capabilities, including the development of rockets and other weaponry. Understanding the Iran-Hamas relationship is vital for comprehending the organization's military capabilities and regional alliances.

The relationship between Iran and Hamas has been a significant factor in shaping the organization's activities and its role in regional politics. Iran has provided support to Hamas, particularly in terms of funding, weapons, and training.

Iran's support for Hamas has been a major game-changer, hasn't it? Their shared anti-Israel sentiments and religious ties have solidified this relationship. Iran's backing has significantly contributed to Hamas's military capabilities. They've provided funding, weapons, and training, which have allowed Hamas to develop a formidable arsenal, including rockets and other weaponry.

Iran's involvement in the region's politics through its support for Hamas has had far-reaching consequences. It's not just about military aid; it also influences the broader dynamics of the Israeli-Palestinian conflict. Therefore, Iran's involvement certainly adds another layer of complexity to the Middle East's geopolitical landscape. It underscores the interconnectedness of regional alliances and how they impact the activities and strategies of groups like Hamas.

Here are some examples of the Iran-Hamas relationship:

1. **Financial Support:** Iran has been a key source of financial assistance to Hamas. This support has enabled the organization to maintain its operations, including funding social services and conducting military activities.

2. **Weapons and Training**: Iran has supplied Hamas with weapons, including rockets and other armaments. Iranian experts have also provided training to members of Hamas's military wing, the Izz ad-Din al-Qassam Brigades.

3. **Political Backing**: Iran has offered political support to Hamas, recognizing it as a legitimate Palestinian resistance movement. This backing has elevated Hamas's international profile and provided it with a degree of legitimacy in certain circles.

4. **Geopolitical Considerations**: Iran's support for Hamas is partly driven by its geopolitical interests. By assisting Hamas, Iran gains influence in the Israeli-Palestinian conflict and a foothold in the Gaza Strip.

5. **Regional Alliances**: The Iran-Hamas relationship intersects with broader regional alliances. Iran's support for Hamas has put it in direct opposition to Israel and its allies, further complicating regional dynamics.

Understanding the Iran-Hamas relationship is essential for comprehending the organization's activities and its role in the broader Middle East. It is a critical aspect of the geopolitical landscape in the region, and it highlights the multifaceted dynamics of the Israeli-Palestinian conflict.

4.1.d Qatar : Diplomatic Backing

Qatar's relationship with Hamas is quite interesting. They've been providing political and financial support to the organization, despite Hamas being considered a terrorist group by some countries, it's a contentious issue. Qatar has welcomed

Hamas leaders and even mediated in conflicts involving the organization, which has raised eyebrows among some of its international partners.

Qatar's position on Hamas is often seen as a reflection of its broader foreign policy in the Middle East. They've tried to balance regional alliances while also maintaining ties with Hamas, which can be a tricky diplomatic feat, and it highlights the complexities of international relations in the region. Qatar's engagement with Hamas has certainly generated mixed reactions and differing views.

Examples of Qatar's relationship with Hamas include:

a. **Political Support**: Qatar has provided a platform for Hamas leaders, allowing them to conduct diplomatic and political activities on its soil.

b. **Mediation** Efforts: Qatar has been involved in mediating negotiations and ceasefire agreements between Hamas and Israel.

c. **Financial Aid**: Qatar has offered financial aid to support various projects in the Gaza Strip, including humanitarian assistance and infrastructure development.

d. **Hosting Hamas Leaders**: Qatar has hosted prominent Hamas leaders, offering them a safe haven and allowing them to engage in international diplomacy.

e. **Al Jazeera Coverage**: The Qatari-owned news network, Al Jazeera, has covered events related to Hamas and the Israeli-Palestinian conflict, often providing a platform for Hamas representatives.

It's important to note that Qatar's relationship with Hamas has been a subject of international debate, with some countries viewing it as problematic due to Hamas's designation as a terrorist organization in their jurisdictions.

4.1e. Turkey and Hamas

Turkey's approach to Hamas is quite interesting, isn't it? On one hand, they maintain relations with the Palestinian Authority in the West Bank, and on the other, they engage with Hamas in Gaza, it's definitely a nuanced diplomatic stance. Turkey's engagement with Hamas has been a point of contention. Some argue that it's a pragmatic move to have a role in the Gaza Strip, while others see it as lending legitimacy to a group that's designated as a terrorist organization by some countries.

Turkey frames its engagement with Hamas as a means to contribute to the Palestinian cause and promote reconciliation. But critics argue that it complicates the already challenging Israel-Palestine situation. It's a delicate balancing act for Turkey. They want to play a role in the region and support the Palestinian people, but it does create differing perspectives and concerns about the country's approach to Hamas.

Examples of Turkey's relationship with Hamas include:

a. **Diplomatic Engagement**: Turkey has hosted meetings and discussions involving Hamas leaders and has served as a mediator between Hamas and other parties in the region.

b. **Humanitarian Aid**: Turkey has provided humanitarian assistance to the Palestinian territories, including Gaza, which has indirectly benefited the Hamas-controlled administration.

c. **Criticisms and Concerns**: Turkey has faced criticism from some countries for its engagement with Hamas, as it is designated as a terrorist organization by the European Union and others. This has caused tensions with some of Turkey's international allies.

Turkey's stance on Hamas reflects its broader foreign policy objectives in the Middle East and its support for Palestinian self-determination. However, it has also generated controversy and disagreements with other countries regarding its relationship with the organization.

4.1f. Lebanon relation with Hamas

Lebanon's relationship with Hamas is influenced by various factors, including the complex political landscape of Lebanon and the Palestinian refugee population in the country. Here are some key points regarding Lebanon's relationship with Hamas:

a. **Palestinian Refugee Camps**: Lebanon is home to several Palestinian refugee camps, and the living conditions in these camps have often been challenging. Palestinian factions, including Hamas, have a presence in some of these camps.

b. **Lebanese Politics**: The presence of Palestinian factions, including Hamas, in Lebanon has at times been a source of political tension. The Lebanese government has had to navigate the dynamics of Palestinian factions within its borders.

c. **Support and Activities**: Hamas has engaged in political and social activities within Palestinian refugee camps in Lebanon, including offering services and advocating for the rights of Palestinian refugees.

d. **Political Considerations**: Lebanon's relationship with Hamas is influenced by the broader regional politics and alliances in the Middle East. This relationship can be affected by the stance of different Lebanese political groups and their alignment with regional actors.

It's important to note that the relationship between Lebanon and Hamas is just one aspect of Lebanon's complex political and social landscape, and it can be influenced by a wide range of factors.

Western Relations: The Quartet and Diplomatic Isolation

Hamas's stance on Israel, its use of violence, and its Islamist ideology have led to its diplomatic isolation in many Western countries. The Quartet on the Middle East, composed of the United States, the European Union, Russia, and the United Nations, has articulated conditions for engaging with Hamas. This chapter explores the diplomatic challenges Hamas faces on the international stage and its impact on the Israeli-Palestinian peace process.

Arab States and the Arab-Israeli Conflict

Hamas's role in the Israeli-Palestinian conflict has repercussions for the broader Arab-Israeli conflict and the Arab states' relations with Israel. The stance of Arab countries on Hamas's activities and its influence on the peace process is an essential aspect of understanding the regional dynamics.

4.2   Hamas and Israel: Direct and Indirect Relations

Indeed, the relationship between Hamas and Israel has been highly contentious for many years. It's a complex situation, to say the least. Because, the conflict has deep historical roots especially related to the religious site claim and has resulted in numerous violent clashes. There have been periods of relative calm, but they've often been short-lived., and there's a constant struggle to maintain any kind of lasting ceasefire agreement. It's a delicate balance that often gets disrupted.

The issue of direct and indirect interactions is crucial here. Sometimes it's through intermediaries, like Egypt or the United Nations, while other times, it's direct confrontations along the border. However, it's not just a military conflict; there are political, economic, and humanitarian dimensions to this as well. It affects the lives of countless people in the region, and it's a situation with far-reaching implications not just for Israel and Gaza but for the broader Middle East. It's a topic that demands continuous attention and international efforts to find a peaceful resolution.

Direct Conflict: Direct clashes between Hamas and the Israel Defense Forces (IDF) have resulted in numerous casualties and significant damage. The organization's military activities, including rocket attacks and border clashes, have been met with Israeli military responses. Understanding the dynamics of these direct confrontations is essential to appreciating the on-ground realities in the Israeli-Palestinian conflict.

Indirect Negotiations and Ceasefires: Hamas and Israel have engaged in indirect negotiations and ceasefire agreements, often brokered by third parties like Egypt and Qatar. These negotiations have aimed to reduce hostilities and establish periods of calm in the Gaza Strip. Examining these diplomatic efforts provides insights into the possibilities of long-term truce and peaceful coexistence.

4.3. The United Nations and International Organizations

Hamas's interactions with the United Nations (UN) and other international organizations are pivotal in shaping its diplomatic presence and aspirations.

UN Recognition: The Palestinian Authority, led by Fatah, has sought recognition as a non-member observer state in the UN. While this endeavor is primarily associated with the Palestinian Authority, Hamas's stance on the matter and its implications for the organization are discussed in this section.

Humanitarian Aid and NGOs: Hamas has had interactions with humanitarian organizations and non-governmental organizations (NGOs) that provide aid and services in the Gaza Strip. The presence of these organizations has implications for the local population and the organization's governance in the region.

The Role of Diaspora Palestinians and the Palestinian Diaspora

Hamas's influence extends to the Palestinian diaspora, including Palestinians living in various countries worldwide. Understanding how the organization interacts with these communities and how diaspora Palestinians support or engage with Hamas is integral to comprehending its global reach.

Hamas's Efforts for International Recognition

Hamas has sought international recognition and legitimacy despite its classification as a terrorist organization by some countries. This section explores the organization's diplomatic initiatives and its impact on its standing on the global stage.

Challenges and Opportunities

Hamas's regional and international relations are fraught with both challenges and opportunities. The organization faces diplomatic isolation in many Western countries due to its use of violence and its stance on Israel. However, it has received support from countries in the Middle East and beyond that share its anti-Israel sentiments. This chapter dissects the complexities of these relations and their implications for Hamas's strategies and the Israeli-Palestinian conflict as a whole.

Understanding the intricate web of regional and international relations in which Hamas is embedded is essential for gaining insights into the organization's activities, policies, and its role in the broader context of the Israeli-Palestinian conflict. These relations are ever-evolving and dynamic, shaping the organization's strategies and its potential impact on the path to peace in the Middle East..

Chapter 5: Hamas and Civilian Shields

In the tumult of the Israel-Palestine conflict, a disturbing practice stains the battleground—the deliberate use of human shields by various Palestinian organizations in the Gaza Strip like, Hamas, The Islamic Jihad Movement in Palestine and The Popular Resistance Committees (PRC) This troubling tactics of these extremist organisation favored by violent extremists, adds layers of complexity and moral quandaries to an already charged conflict. Both defensively and offensively, Palestinian groups intertwine civilians with military operations, turning them into involuntary participants in a high stakes geopolitical struggle.

This intentional deployment of human shields not only imperils innocent lives but also raises profound ethical concerns within the theater of warfare. It vividly illustrates the asymmetrical dynamics of the conflict, where non-combatants find themselves unwittingly thrust into the midst of broader geopolitical maneuvers.

As the Israel-Palestine conflict rages on, the persistent use of human shields amplifies an already explosive situation, prompting scrutiny regarding compliance with international humanitarian law. Confronting this issue becomes imperative for cultivating a more ethically grounded approach to conflict resolution and safeguarding the vulnerable civilian populations ensnared in the crossfire. The prevalence of such tactics underscores the pressing need for a comprehensive and equitable resolution to the protracted Israel-Palestine conflict, casting a critical light on the complexities that define this enduring struggle.

5.1 Hamas and Civilian Shields

In 2007, reports emerged revealing Hamas's utilization of the "Civilian shield" strategy as a defensive weapon against Israeli military operations. This tactic sparked numerous human rights concerns as the lives of civilians were placed in imminent danger. The complex ethical implications surrounding Hamas's approach raised alarms within the international community. This strategy, could serve Hamas not just as a military ploy but also as a legal maneuver. It provides them with the opportunity to accuse Israel of committing war crimes, potentially resulting in the imposition of various sanctions. This dual nature of utilizing civilians both as shields and as potential legal leverage underscores the intricate and contentious dynamics at play in the Israel-Palestine conflict.

5.1a How Hamas uses Civilian Shields:

(1) One of Hamas's effective strategies against Israel is rocket attacks. They launch rockets, artillery, and mortars from or near densely populated civilian areas, including schools, hospitals, or mosques, which are supposed to be safeguarded under the Geneva Convention. Hamas exploits the loopholes in this law, using civilian areas for their attacks against Israel.

(2) Placing military and security-related infrastructures like headquarters, bases, armories, access routes, and defensive positions within or near civilian areas is a concerning practice. This strategy, often employed by various entities, poses significant risks to civilian populations. The proximity of essential military facilities to civilian hubs creates potential dangers, making civilians vulnerable to collateral damage during conflicts. This tactic blurs the lines between military and civilian spaces, increasing the potential for unintended harm to non-combatants. It underscores the complex ethical challenges in modern warfare, where the positioning of military assets can have far-reaching consequences on civilian safety and well-being.

(3) Shielding terrorists' residences and military installations, or orchestrating rescues for besieged or warned terrorists by the IDF, raises grave ethical and security concerns. Such actions not only jeopardize the safety of civilians but also hinder legitimate military operations aimed at maintaining

security. By intertwining terrorists with civilian infrastructure, this strategy exploits humanitarian principles, placing innocent lives at risk. It underscores the challenges in counterterrorism efforts, where tactics that blur the lines between combatants and non-combatants further complicate the delicate balance between national security and humanitarian considerations.

Engaging the IDF from or near residential and commercial areas, coupled with the use of civilians for intelligence gathering missions, represents a perilous strategy with far-reaching consequences. This tactic deliberately places civilians at the heart of conflict zones, exposing them to the inherent dangers of warfare. By intertwining military activities with civilian spaces, armed groups not only compromise the safety of non-combatants but also exploit their presence for strategic advantage.

The deployment of civilians for intelligence gathering further exacerbates the ethical complexities. Civilians, inadvertently turned into informants, face heightened risks as they navigate the precarious terrain between conflicting forces. This blurring of lines between combatants and non-combatants challenges established norms of warfare, raising critical questions about the protection of civilian lives in conflict zones.

This strategy not only endangers innocent lives but also hampers the IDF's ability to respond effectively to security threats. It underscores the urgent need for a reassessment of tactics that put civilians in harm's way, emphasizing the intricate balance between national security imperatives and the protection of civilian populations in the midst of conflict. Addressing this challenge is crucial for fostering a more secure and ethically sound approach to conflict resolution.

5.1b Evidence of Hamas using Civilian Shields against Israel

(1) May 2004 :   An ambulance labeled with a UN designation was employed for transporting Hamas combatants. (Reference: Channel 10 (Israel)-24 May 2004

(2) October 2006:   IDF soldiers discovered ammunition in a residential building. (Reference: IDF Spokesman)

(3) 20 November 2006: Hamas urged civilians to ascend to the rooftop of a Hamas executive's residence in response to the IDF's early warning. (Reference: ANB TV,20 November 2006).

(4) 12 June 2007: An unintended explosion occurred while assembling an improvised explosive device (IED) within a residential house, resulting in the collapse of the structure. The incident led to the tragic loss of 10 civilian lives and left 40 others injured. (Reference: Al-Hayat newspaper, 14 June 2007).

(5) 2008: Machinery, specifically lathes, employed for the manufacturing of weapons and ammunition, situated either within or in close proximity to residential areas. (Reference: IDF Spokesman).

(6) 2008:   Entry and exit points of tunnels situated within residential homes. (Reference: IDF Spokesman).

(7) 29 January 2008: A facility for the production of rockets was found within a residential dwelling in the northern region of the Gaza Strip. (Reference: Der Spiegel newspaper, 30 January 2008).

(8) August 2008: Hamas' Special Forces conduct training in the streets of the Tufah neighborhood in Gaza. (Reference: Palestine Info Center, 20 August 2008).

(9) 2 January 2009: A mosque served as the headquarters and armory for Hamas. (Reference: IDF Spokesman, 2 January 2009).

(10) 28 January 2009: In the initial week of Operation Cast Lead, the IDF targeted Hamas' Research and Development center situated at the Islamic University in Gaza. (Reference: IDF Spokesman, December 28 2009; Al-Aqsa TV,28 December 2009).

(11) July 2014: Following the IDF's early warning, civilians ascended to the rooftop of a Hamas executive's residence. (Reference: Alwatan TV, 9 July 2014)

5.1c Chronology of Significant Events

(1) 14 June 2007: Hamas took complete control of the Gaza Strip.

(2) December 2008 – 18 January 2009: Gaza War (Operation Cast Lead), a three-week armed conflict involving

Palestinians in the Gaza Strip and Israel. Israel's official objective is to halt indiscriminate Palestinian rocket attacks into Israel and weapons smuggling into the Gaza Strip. The conflict leads to the deaths of over 1,000 people, predominantly Palestinians. The IDF adopts the practice of "roof knocking" to warn residents before an attack, aiming to minimize civilian casualties. There is an increase in the use of human shields by Hamas.

(3) 15 September 2009: The UN Fact-Finding Mission on the Gaza Conflict, led by Judge Richard Goldstone, releases the "Goldstone Report," accusing both the IDF and Palestinian militants of war crimes and potential crimes against humanity during the Gaza War.

(4) 24 September 2009: The Israeli government issues an initial 32-point formal response to the Goldstone Report.

(5) November 2009: The U.S. House of Representatives overwhelmingly passes a resolution, declaring the Goldstone Report irredeemably biased and unworthy of further consideration or legitimacy.

(6) 10 March 2010: The European Parliament passes a resolution endorsing the Goldstone Report.

(7) 31 May 2010: Gaza flotilla raid: Israeli naval commandos forcefully halt six civilian ships attempting to break the Israeli blockade of the Gaza Strip. Ten Turkish activists die.

(8) March 2012: Operation Returning Echo, a five-day IDF operation in the Gaza Strip primarily consisting of targeted air strikes. Hamas responds with rocket attacks on Israel.

(9) 14–21 November 2012 Operation Pillar of Defense, an eight-day IDF operation in the Gaza Strip. The Israeli military eliminates key militant leaders of Hamas and destroys weapons and bases.

(10) 8 July – 26 August 2014: Israel-Gaza Conflict (Operation Protective Edge), a seven-week Israeli military operation in the Gaza Strip with the stated aim of ending Hamas rocket fire. The conflict results in the deaths of over 2,000 people, predominantly Palestinians. Israel launches a comprehensive program encouraging local officials to evacuate civilians before conducting military strikes against Hamas.

5.1d: Navigating the Shadows: Hamas, Civilian Shields, and the Tunnel Economy

In the intricate dance of conflict in the Gaza Strip, Hamas has strategically utilized the shielding of civilians as a tactical advantage. By operating within civilian areas, the organization seeks a protected zone, capitalizing on the dilemma faced by the Israel Defense Forces (IDF). Targeted strikes on areas functioning as Hamas hubs inevitably put civilian lives at risk, providing a shield of protection for the group.

While the use of human shields may not have direct economic implications, the underbelly of this strategy reveals a complex web of clandestine activities. Hamas recruits and compensates civilians for tunnel construction, weaving an intricate network beneath the surface. Tunnels, particularly concentrated in the Rafah border town near Egypt, serve as vital conduits for revenue, commodities, arms, and recruits for Hamas, numbering between 400 to 600 by various estimates. The majority of these tunnels are directly operated by Hamas, with civilian operators of the remainder taxed by the Hamas government.

Despite the apparent economic benefits for the local population, those involved in tunnel construction face perilous conditions. Accidents, most notably tunnel collapses, pose a constant threat to the lives of these civilians, who also become more susceptible to IDF attacks.

This dual-purpose tactic of civilian infrastructure use not only complicates IDF responses but also blurs the line between civilian and military objectives. The IDF, constrained by the difficulty of distinguishing between "civilian" criminal usage and "military" operations, faces a challenging landscape in countering these underground networks.

Hamas further exploits the aftermath of conflict, leveraging damage to civilians and infrastructure to garner funds for reconstruction. Donor nations, including Qatar and Turkey, are solicited to aid in rebuilding, but reports abound of diverted funds meant for reconstruction finding their way into the coffers of Hamas's armed wing.

In the shadows of the Gaza conflict, the intricate interplay of civilian shields, tunnel economies, and reconstruction funds paints a complex picture of the strategic maneuvers employed by Hamas, offering a glimpse into the multifaceted nature of this enduring conflict.

5.1e: Hamas's Legal Chess: Turning Law into a Battlefield

In the game of conflict, Hamas has a sneaky move up its sleeve — a strategy called lawfare. Knowing Israel's got the upper hand in military might, Hamas plays a legal card by using human shields, turning international laws into a weapon.

Here's the trick: If Israel goes all out with big firepower, causing lots of civilian harm, Hamas points fingers and cries war crimes. This can lead to serious consequences, like sanctions against Israel. But if Israel tries to be careful and avoid hurting civilians, Hamas stays safe while still fighting.

Hamas is no slouch when it comes to gathering evidence, especially when bad stuff happens. During past operations, they teamed up with different groups to collect info about what they claim are Israel's war crimes. They then take these complaints to courts in Europe.

Why does this matter? Well, Hamas knows that accusing Israel of breaking the rules, like the Geneva Convention, gets them in trouble internationally. It's like a reputation hit for Israel. And here's the twist — Hamas is smart about dragging out these legal fights. By making it a long process, they keep the pressure on and keep Israel's reputation in hot water.

So, in this complex game of law and conflict, Hamas is playing its cards right, using legal moves to make things tricky for Israel on the world stage.

5.2 The Palestinian Islamic Jihad (PIJ

The Palestinian Islamic Jihad (PIJ), established in 1981, operates under the guise of the Islamic Jihad Movement in Palestine. This Palestinian Islamist terror organization explicitly seeks the annihilation of the State of Israel, aspiring to establish a sovereign Islamic Palestinian state. Disturbingly, the PIJ has been implicated in employing civilians as shields in its operational strategies. This reprehensible tactic places innocent lives at risk and further underscores the complexities of asymmetrical warfare in the Israel-Palestine conflict. The use of civilian shields not only endangers the lives of non-combatants but also adds a layer of ethical concern to the activities of this extremist group. The international community closely monitors such practices, emphasizing the imperative for a comprehensive and just resolution to the enduring challenges in the region.

5.2a How "The Palestinian Islamic Jihad is different from Hams?

The Palestinian Islamic Jihad (PIJ) and Hamas are distinct Islamist organizations, each with its own ideologies, structures, and objectives. Here are key differences between the two:

1. Founding and Background:

- PIJ: Established in 1981 during the early years of the First Intifada, PIJ is a more recent addition to the Palestinian political landscape compared to Hamas.

- Hamas: Founded in 1987, Hamas emerged during the First Intifada as well, but it predates PIJ by a few years.

2. Objectives:

- PIJ: PIJ is known for its uncompromising stance on the complete destruction of the State of Israel and the establishment of an independent Palestinian state.

- Hamas: While also advocating for Palestinian statehood, Hamas has a more complex and nuanced political approach. It has participated in Palestinian elections and has both a military and a political wing.

3. Leadership and Structure:

- PIJ: Traditionally, PIJ has had a more centralized structure with a strong leadership.

- Hamas: Hamas has a multifaceted structure, with a political bureau and a military wing. It has also been involved in Palestinian governance.

4. International Relations:

- PIJ: PIJ is generally considered more ideologically rigid and has fewer international connections compared to Hamas.

- Hamas: While also having a strong ideological foundation, Hamas has engaged in diplomatic efforts and has received varying degrees of support from different countries in the region.

5. Approach to Ceasefires:

- PIJ: PIJ has often been less willing to adhere to ceasefires and has been involved in more sporadic and intense conflicts with Israel.

- Hamas: While engaging in conflicts, Hamas has also entered into ceasefires and truces with Israel at various times.

While both organizations share a commitment to the Palestinian cause, their strategies, political engagement, and relationships with other actors in the region differ significantly.

5.3. Popular Resistance Committees (PRC): Defiance and Militancy in Gaza

In the complex tapestry of Palestinian factions, the Popular Resistance Committees (PRC) emerge as a coalition of armed groups united by their opposition to what they perceive as the Palestinian Authority and Fatah's conciliatory stance towards Israel. Founded on the bedrock of resistance, the PRC wields influence, particularly in the tumultuous Gaza Strip, primarily through its military arm, the Al-Nasser Salah al-Deen Brigades.

The PRC's distinctive stance reflects the broader ideological schisms within the Palestinian territories, as it navigates the intricate landscape of resistance politics. With a fervent commitment to challenging the status quo, the PRC has become a key player in shaping the narrative of Palestinian resistance, carving its presence through both rhetoric and actions.

However, beneath the surface of their militant activities lies a controversial and morally fraught tactic – the use of civilian shields against Israel. Facts indicate that the PRC, like other factions, has strategically employed civilians in proximity to military operations, effectively turning them into inadvertent shields. This reprehensible strategy not only endangers the lives of non-combatants but also seeks to exploit the ethical complexities of engaging with a formidable adversary.

The deliberate intertwining of military activities with civilian populations not only poses a severe violation of international humanitarian law but also underscores the challenges faced by Israel in navigating a conflict landscape where the boundaries between combatants and non-combatants blur. As international scrutiny intensifies, the actions of the PRC highlight the urgent need for a comprehensive and just resolution to the enduring challenges that define the Israel-Palestine conflict. The nuanced dance between resistance and militancy in Gaza continues, leaving an indelible mark on the region's turbulent history.

5.3a How "The Popular Resistance Committees (PRC)" is different from Hams?

The Popular Resistance Committees (PRC) and Hamas are distinct Palestinian groups, each with its own history, objectives, and methods. Here are key differences between the Popular Resistance Committees and Hamas:

1. Founding and Background:

- PRC: The Popular Resistance Committees are a coalition of various armed Palestinian groups formed in 2000 during the

Second Intifada. They are not a single, unified organization but rather an alliance with different factions.

- Hamas: Founded in 1987, Hamas is a well-established Palestinian Islamist organization that originated during the First Intifada.

2. Objectives:

- PRC: The PRC's objectives may vary among its constituent factions, but it generally opposes what it perceives as a conciliatory approach by the Palestinian Authority and Fatah towards Israel.

- Hamas: Hamas explicitly seeks the establishment of an independent Palestinian state and the resistance against Israeli occupation. It has both political and military wings.

3. Structure:

- PRC: The PRC is more of a loose coalition without a centralized leadership structure.

- Hamas: Hamas has a well-defined organizational structure with a political bureau and a military wing.

4. Engagement in Governance:

- PRC: The PRC is not primarily engaged in political governance and does not have the same political role as Hamas.

- Hamas: In addition to its military activities, Hamas has been involved in Palestinian politics and has gained political power, particularly in the Gaza Strip.

5. International Recognition:

- PRC: The PRC does not enjoy the same level of international recognition as Hamas.

- Hamas: Hamas has faced international controversy, with some countries labeling it a terrorist organization, while others, especially in the Arab world, recognize its political legitimacy.

While both groups are involved in resistance activities against Israel, their structures, objectives, and levels of international recognition differ significantly.

Chapter 6: Conflict and Peace Efforts

Diving into the world of diplomatic dance between Hamas and Israel, it's like trying to solve a puzzle with many missing pieces. They've tried a bunch of ways to find a solution, but it's not as easy as it sounds.

One big hurdle is Jerusalem – both sides want a piece of it, and agreeing on who gets what is like trying to share a pizza with uneven toppings. Then there's the refugee crisis, a bit like trying to fix a jigsaw puzzle without all the right pieces.

And let's not forget the security stuff – everyone wants to feel safe, but figuring out how to make that happen without stepping on each other's toes is a challenge.

As they continue this diplomatic dance, these big problems keep getting in the way. It's like trying to waltz through a maze. Getting to a solution is tricky, and it needs both Hamas and Israel to bring their A-game to make it work. The journey to a peaceful agreement is a bumpy ride, and it's going to take some clever moves to get there.

6.1 The Annapolis Conference: A Hopeful Start

The Annapolis Conference was a diplomatic gathering held in November 2007 in Annapolis, Maryland, USA. It aimed to revive the Israeli-Palestinian peace process, which had stagnated for several years. The conference brought together key figures from Israel and the Palestinian Authority, as well as representatives from other countries in the region and international organizations.

Hosted by then-U.S. President George W. Bush, the conference sought to address core issues of the Israeli-Palestinian conflict, including borders, the status of Jerusalem, the fate of Palestinian refugees, and security arrangements. The goal was to restart negotiations and lay the groundwork for a two-state solution, where Israel and a future independent Palestinian state would coexist peacefully.

While there was initial optimism surrounding the conference, subsequent events revealed the challenges and deep-seated issues that persisted in the region. The Annapolis Conference did lead to a series of negotiations, but a comprehensive peace agreement remained elusive. The complexities of the Israeli-Palestinian conflict, coupled with shifts in political dynamics, hindered the sustained progress that many had hoped for following the conference.

Result from Annapolis Conference:

The idea of this conference was like, "Hey, maybe this is the moment things will finally change."

But, here's the twist: it didn't quite turn out that way. Even though there was a lot of hope at the beginning, the tough issues that caused problems before were still hanging around. The Annapolis Conference, in the end, felt more like a quick burst of fireworks than a lasting solution for peace.

What happened there showed us that fixing the long-standing problems in the Middle East needs more than just a big meeting. It's like trying to solve a puzzle that's been tricky for a really long time. The Annapolis try was a bit like a rollercoaster – some ups, some downs, but not the smooth ride everyone hoped for.

So, what's the takeaway? Well, the Annapolis Conference teaches us that the path to peace in the Middle East is a bit like a bumpy road. It's going to take more than one conference to figure it all out, and there's still a lot of work to do to untangle the mess. The story of making peace in the Middle East is still unfolding, and Annapolis is just one chapter in the bigger picture.

6.2 Intermittent Talks Facilitated by Egypt: Diplomacy in Action

"Intermittent Talks Facilitated by Egypt: Diplomacy in Action" likely refers to diplomatic efforts involving discussions or negotiations facilitated by Egypt to address certain issues or conflicts. The term "intermittent talks" suggests that these discussions occur periodically or with breaks in between.

In a diplomatic context, countries or parties may engage in talks facilitated by a third-party mediator, in this case, Egypt. These talks could cover a range of topics, such as resolving regional conflicts, addressing political differences, or finding solutions to specific challenges.

The phrase "Diplomacy in Action" emphasizes the active and ongoing nature of diplomatic efforts. It suggests that nations are actively engaging in dialogue, negotiations, or discussions to navigate through complex issues. Egypt, as the facilitator, plays a role in mediating and fostering communication between the involved parties.

The effectiveness of such diplomatic endeavors depends on the willingness of the parties involved to find common ground and work towards mutually beneficial solutions. Overall, the term reflects a diplomatic process aimed at resolving issues through dialogue and negotiation.

Deep-rooted Issues: A Persistent Challenge

In the ongoing saga of the Israel-Palestine conflict, certain issues prove to be stubborn knots resisting easy untangling. Take Jerusalem, a city not just made of stone but infused with deep religious and cultural significance. It's a focal point of contention, where every cobblestone carries the weight of historical disputes.

Then comes the refugee dilemma, a complex tale of people displaced through time. It's not just about homes left behind; it's a web of narratives, dreams shattered, and a longing that transcends generations. This adds layers of complexity to an already intricate negotiation landscape.

Amidst all this, the haunting specter of security concerns is an ever-present companion. It's not just a talking point; it's the heartbeat of daily life, pulsating with fears that echo on both sides of the divide. This isn't just politics; it's the lived experience of people who grapple with the very real implications of their leaders' decisions.

Picture diplomats sitting across tables; these issues loom large, defying straightforward solutions. Each attempt at resolution becomes a high-stakes dance, navigating historical, cultural, and emotional minefields. It's a journey towards understanding and compromise, fraught with pitfalls but necessary for any hope of a shared future. The question lingers:

Can the echoes of history and the weight of the present be unraveled for the sake of peace? The dance of negotiations continues, against the backdrop of ancient walls and the complexities of the modern world. Only time will reveal the next steps in this delicate waltz.

Conclusion: Navigating the Thorny Path

In the intricate dance of conflict in the Gaza Strip, Hamas has strategically utilized the shielding of civilians as a tactical advantage. By operating within civilian areas, the organization seeks a protected zone, capitalizing on the dilemma faced by the Israel Defense Forces (IDF). Targeted strikes on areas functioning as Hamas hubs inevitably put civilian lives at risk, providing a shield of protection for the group.

While the use of human shields may not have direct economic implications, the underbelly of this strategy reveals a complex web of clandestine activities. Hamas recruits and compensates civilians for tunnel construction, weaving an intricate network beneath the surface. Tunnels, particularly concentrated in the Rafah border town near Egypt, serve as vital conduits for revenue, commodities, arms, and recruits for Hamas, numbering between 400 to 600 by various estimates. The majority of these tunnels are directly operated by Hamas, with civilian operators of the remainder taxed by the Hamas government.

Despite the apparent economic benefits for the local population, those involved in tunnel construction face perilous conditions. Accidents, most notably tunnel collapses, pose a constant threat to the lives of these civilians, who also become more susceptible to IDF attacks.

This dual-purpose tactic of civilian infrastructure use not only complicates IDF responses but also blurs the line between civilian and military objectives. The IDF, constrained by the difficulty of distinguishing between "civilian" criminal usage and "military" operations, faces a challenging landscape in countering these underground networks.

Hamas further exploits the aftermath of conflict, leveraging damage to civilians and infrastructure to garner funds for reconstruction. Donor nations, including Qatar and Turkey, are solicited to aid in rebuilding, but reports abound of diverted funds meant for reconstruction finding their way into the coffers of Hamas's armed wing.

In the shadows of the Gaza conflict, the intricate interplay of civilian shields, tunnel economies, and reconstruction funds paints a complex picture of the strategic maneuvers employed by Hamas, offering a glimpse into the multifaceted nature of this enduring conflict.

Chapter 7: Nexus between Iran-Hezbollah and Hamas

7.1 Iran-Hamas alliance

In examining the roots of the Iran-Hamas alliance, a crucial dimension unveils itself — a purposeful alignment of ideologies. This strategic partnership is not happenstance; rather, it stems from a deliberate and shared fervor opposing Israel and an unwavering commitment to the Palestinian cause. This alignment provides a solid foundation, a common ground upon which the strategic collaboration between Iran and Hamas is meticulously constructed.

The ideological resonance between these entities forms the bedrock of their alliance. Both share a profound opposition to Israeli policies and occupation, underscoring their commitment to championing the Palestinian cause. This alignment isn't merely symbolic; it translates into a strategic framework that shapes their collective objectives and actions.

As the Iran-Hamas alliance navigates the complexities of the Middle East, this ideological nexus serves as a guiding force. It manifests not only in their joint opposition to a common adversary but also in the pursuit of a shared vision for the Palestinian people. This purposeful alignment lays bare the intricate tapestry of their strategic collaboration, where ideology becomes a driving force, shaping the contours of their geopolitical engagement in the region.

7.1a Financial Support to Hamas as a Strategic Tool

Iran provides substantial financial support to Hamas, signaling a deep-rooted alliance in their shared pursuit of the Palestinian cause. This collaboration extends beyond mere rhetoric, as widely reported in international news. The financial backing from Iran is a strategic lifeline for Hamas, enabling the group to sustain its operational capabilities and solidify its stronghold in the Gaza Strip.

The infusion of funds serves as a critical tool for both parties, advancing their collective agenda with calculated precision. In the intricate geopolitical landscape of the Middle East, this financial support from Iran plays a pivotal role in shaping the power dynamics surrounding the Hamas-Israel conflict.

Hamas, designated as a terrorist organization by several countries, benefits significantly from this backing, allowing it to navigate the complex challenges posed by its adversaries.

Iran's strategic investment not only fortifies Hamas militarily but also bolsters its political standing, providing the group with the means to influence regional dynamics.

The financial relationship between Iran and Hamas underscores the interconnected nature of geopolitical interests in the Middle East. As both entities navigate the volatile terrain of the Israeli-Palestinian conflict, the financial support from Iran remains a key factor influencing the trajectory of events. This alliance sheds light on the multifaceted strategies employed by state and non-state actors alike in pursuit of their geopolitical objectives in the region.

7.1b Military Collaboration: Real-Time Impacts

Iran and Hamas are suspected to have a close military collaboration, involving the transfer of weaponry, training, and technological support. Multiple international reports on conflicts involving Hamas suggest real-time impacts of this military alliance. The alignment of their ideologies appears to manifest in joint military actions, bolstering Hamas's military capabilities. This collaboration highlights the intricate interconnectedness of geopolitical interests in the Middle East. The strategic partnership between Iran and Hamas significantly influences the dynamics of the Hamas-Israel conflict, shaping events on the ground.

This military alliance raises concerns about the external influence shaping the trajectory of regional conflicts. As Iran extends support to Hamas, it not only reinforces the group's military capabilities but also deepens the complexity of the broader Middle East geopolitical landscape.

The collaboration goes beyond conventional military aid; it involves the exchange of tactics, strategies, and technological know-how. Reports from the field indicate instances where Hamas has employed military techniques that mirror those used by Iranian-backed militias in other conflicts.

This alignment, however, is not without controversy. The support from Iran provides Hamas with a lifeline, sustaining its operations and fortifying its position in the Gaza Strip. Simultaneously, it contributes to the perpetuation of the Israel-Palestine conflict, as Hamas remains a key player in the region's volatile dynamics.

The shared military endeavors also underscore a broader pattern of alliances in the Middle East, where ideological affinities often dictate strategic partnerships. The Iran-Hamas collaboration is part of a larger tapestry of relationships that shape the power dynamics in the region.

As these collaborations continue to evolve, their implications extend far beyond the immediate theater of conflict. The alignment of Iran and Hamas in military matters not only impacts the ongoing Hamas-Israel conflict but also has wider implications for regional stability and the intricate web of alliances and enmities in the Middle East. The unfolding narrative suggests that the dynamics of this collaboration will play a pivotal role in shaping the future of the region, with consequences that reach beyond the borders of Israel and Gaza.

7.1c Diplomatic Support to Hamas by Iran

In the world of geopolitics, Iran's backing of Hamas goes beyond just money and weaponry—it extends to the diplomatic stage. Picture it as a tag team, where Iran and Hamas join forces to make their voices heard on the global platform.

Their diplomatic collaboration isn't about fancy meetings in grand halls but rather about making strong statements together. Whenever something goes down in the Israeli-Palestinian saga, Iran and Hamas are quick to express their joint opinions, standing shoulder to shoulder against what they perceive as shared challenges.

This synchronized approach isn't just for show. It's a strategic move, a way to tell the world that they're in this together. Coordinated condemnations and united stances amplify the impact of their shared beliefs, making a louder statement on the international scene.

Their diplomatic teamwork isn't just about words—it's a storytelling strategy. Iran and Hamas use diplomatic channels to weave a narrative about the Israeli-Palestinian conflict that aligns with their shared ideology. It's like crafting a tale where they play the heroes fighting a common enemy.

For Iran, supporting Hamas diplomatically isn't just a diplomatic gesture; it's a key part of their broader strategy. By standing with Hamas on the world stage, Iran not only boosts Hamas's global standing but also helps shape the larger narrative around the Israeli-Palestinian conflict. It's a diplomatic dance with political storytelling at its heart, where every move aims to strengthen their collective position.

Global Scrutiny

The alignment of ideologies between Iran and Hamas has garnered significant international attention. News headlines and diplomatic responses from nations critical of Iran's regional influence shed light on the global scrutiny facing this alliance. The evidence of their shared fervor shaping geopolitical dynamics extends beyond regional borders, becoming a subject of debate and concern on the global stage.

In navigating this shared fervor, the Iran-Hamas alliance transforms from an ideological alignment into a geopolitical force with tangible consequences. The evidence, drawn from international news sources, offers a nuanced understanding of how their commitment to a common cause shapes their collaboration in the realms of finance, military strategy, and global diplomacy.

7.2 Hezbollah Role:

Nestled in the heart of this nexus is Hezbollah, a Shiite political and military organization headquartered in Lebanon. Its central role is multifaceted, extending beyond national borders to become a linchpin in the broader ambitions of the Iran-led alliance.

Hezbollah has been reported to provide various forms of support to Hamas, particularly in the context of their shared goals and opposition to Israel. The support ranges from financial aid to military assistance. It's crucial to note that these activities are widely seen as controversial, and different perspectives exist on the nature and extent of the collaboration between Hezbollah and Hamas.

Financially, Hezbollah has allegedly contributed funds to Hamas, helping the Palestinian group sustain its operations and address socio-economic needs. The military assistance includes the provision of training, weapons, and strategic guidance. This collaboration is rooted in their common objectives, such as resistance against Israel and the promotion of Palestinian causes.

However, it's important to approach such information critically, as the dynamics of the Middle East are complex, and perspectives on these collaborations may differ based on geopolitical stances.

7.2a Financial Support to Hamas by Hezbollah

Hezbollah has been alleged to provide financial aid to Hamas, injecting crucial funds into the Palestinian organization's coffers. This financial assistance plays a pivotal role in enabling Hamas to sustain its operations, govern in Gaza, and address the socio-economic needs of the Palestinian population.

One notable example is the financial backing reportedly provided by Hezbollah during the aftermath of the 2014 Israel-Gaza conflict. Reports suggested that Hezbollah extended financial aid to help Hamas rebuild infrastructure and provide humanitarian assistance in the Gaza Strip.

7.2b Military Assistance

Hezbollah's involvement in supporting Hamas extends beyond financial aid, encompassing military assistance as well. This collaboration includes the transfer of weapons, training programs, and strategic guidance to enhance Hamas's military capabilities.

For instance, there have been claims of Hezbollah sharing its expertise in tunnel construction with Hamas. Tunnels have played a significant role in Hamas's military strategy, providing clandestine pathways for militants and facilitating surprise attacks against Israeli forces.

7.2c Strategic Coordination

Hezbollah and Hamas are known to engage in strategic coordination, aligning their efforts to counter common adversaries. Their collaboration becomes evident during periods of heightened tension, such as the 2006 Lebanon War when both organizations faced off against Israel. During this conflict, Hezbollah and Hamas reportedly exchanged insights and tactics to better confront Israeli forces.

It's essential to note that these allegations and reports are subject to geopolitical narratives and may be viewed differently by various stakeholders. While some see this collaboration as a legitimate resistance against perceived aggression, others view it as a destabilizing force in the region. The complex nature of Middle Eastern geopolitics requires careful consideration of multiple perspectives to form a comprehensive understanding of these dynamics.

Chapter 8: Impact on the Palestinian Territories

In the complex tapestry of the Israeli-Palestinian conflict, the influence of Hamas echoes distinctly across the Palestinian territories, leaving an indelible mark on the Gaza Strip and the West Bank.

8.1 Gaza Strip: Navigating the Complex Landscape

Hamas's governance in the Gaza Strip has been a subject of both scrutiny and support. From the outset, the organization's rise to power in 2007 marked a significant turning point. Critics argue that its rule has perpetuated authoritarianism, limiting political freedoms and dissent. The impact on the local economy, coupled with conflicts with Israel, has contributed to a challenging humanitarian situation. Exploring the nuances of this governance sheds light on the multifaceted dynamics shaping life in the Gaza Strip.

Authoritarianism and Political Constraints

Critics contend that Hamas's rule in Gaza has given rise to an authoritarian regime, curbing political freedoms and stifling dissent. The organization's consolidation of power has, at times, resulted in the suppression of opposition voices. Instances of restrictions on freedom of speech and assembly have been documented, contributing to a climate of political tension within the territory.

Economic Challenges and Humanitarian Strain

The governance of Hamas in Gaza has been intertwined with economic challenges, exacerbated by conflicts with Israel. The region has faced restrictions on the movement of goods and people, impacting trade and commerce. The blockade imposed by Israel, in response to security concerns, has further constrained economic opportunities, leaving many Gazans grappling with unemployment and poverty. This economic strain has played a significant role in shaping the humanitarian situation in the Gaza Strip.

Impact on Local Economy

The intricacies of Hamas's governance involve navigating the economic complexities of a region subjected to geopolitical tensions. The challenges in establishing a robust and sustainable economy within the constraints of the broader conflict have led to a reliance on aid and humanitarian assistance. The economic impact of this governance model is integral to understanding the daily realities faced by the people of Gaza.

Conflict with Israel and Security Dynamics

Conflicts with Israel have been a defining feature of Hamas's governance. The organization's militant activities, including rocket attacks and border skirmishes, have resulted in military responses from Israel. The cyclical pattern of violence has not only claimed lives but has also perpetuated a cycle of insecurity and fear. The complex relationship between Hamas and Israel significantly influences the security dynamics within the Gaza Strip.

Humanitarian Implications

The challenging humanitarian situation in Gaza is a direct consequence of the multifaceted governance landscape. Limited access to basic services, including healthcare and education, has been a persistent concern. The impact on civilians, particularly during periods of heightened tensions, underscores the intricate interplay between political decisions and the well-being of the population.

Exploring Nuances for a Comprehensive Perspective

Navigating the complex landscape of Hamas's governance in the Gaza Strip requires a nuanced examination of political, economic, and security dynamics. Acknowledging the diverse perspectives on these issues is essential for fostering a comprehensive understanding of the challenges faced by Gazans. As discussions surrounding the region continue, a holistic exploration of these nuances is crucial for informed analysis and constructive dialogue.

8.2 West Bank: A Ripple Effect

In the intricate tapestry of Palestinian politics, Hamas's formal political control may be rooted in the Gaza Strip, but its influence extends far beyond geographical boundaries, leaving an indelible mark on the West Bank. This chapter delves into the nuanced dynamics that define how Hamas's ideology and actions reverberate across the political, social, and security landscape of the West Bank.

Political Landscape: A Complex Dance of Ideologies

Hamas's ideological divergence from the Fatah-dominated Palestinian Authority (PA) injects a layer of complexity into the political landscape of the West Bank.

Social Dynamics: Shaping Aspirations and Concerns

Beyond the realm of politics, Hamas's influence shapes the social fabric of the West Bank. The organization's ideological stance resonates within civil society, influencing public discourse and shaping the aspirations and concerns of the Palestinian people.

Security Considerations: Navigating Volatility

Security considerations take center stage that how Hamas's alignment with armed resistance against Israel introduces volatility to the security landscape. The PA, tasked with maintaining law and order, faces the delicate challenge of balancing internal security imperatives with addressing the broader aspirations of the Palestinian population. This intricate dance of security concerns adds another layer to the multifaceted impact of Hamas on the West Bank.

8.3 Conclusion: Beyond Borders

As we dive into the influence of Hamas on the Palestinian territories, it's more than just a political tale—it's a journey through the daily lives of people caught in the crossfire. This isn't about borders; it's about the struggles, dreams, and strength of a community facing the enduring complexities of conflict.

Hamas isn't a distant force confined to political boundaries; it's a living thread woven into the fabric of everyday existence. It shapes the economy, molds education, and leaves its mark on the social and cultural landscape. But this isn't just a story of political decisions; it's about the lives of regular folks in Gaza, the West Bank, and beyond.

Analyzing the consequences reveals that Hamas's role is more than political authority—it's an integral part of people's lives. This narrative is one of complexity, where political choices echo through the daily experiences of ordinary individuals, influencing their dreams, aspirations, and what makes them human.

Beyond the political struggle, this journey through the impact of Hamas is a reminder that prolonged conflict becomes more than just a political fight—it becomes a shared reality. The desire for peace, stability, and a brighter future is universal, crossing political lines.

In the end, exploring Hamas's impact on the Palestinian territories is like unraveling a tapestry of human stories. It's a call for understanding beyond political talk, asking us to connect with the individuals whose lives are deeply intertwined with the ongoing Israeli-Palestinian saga. This is a story that reaches beyond borders—a universal tale of resilience, hope, and the unyielding human spirit in the midst of a lasting struggle.

Chapter 9: Brief profiles of key individuals within Hamas

From founders like Ahmed Yassin, who provided ideological direction, to contemporary leaders like Ismail Haniyeh, navigating the challenges of governance, each individual plays a unique role. The profiles offer insights into the diverse backgrounds and experiences that shape Hamas's multifaceted engagement, encompassing political leadership, diplomatic efforts, and the ongoing resistance against occupation. Some of the key members are:

1. Khaled Mashal

- Role: Former Political Bureau Chief of Hamas.

- Background: Mashal played a pivotal role in shaping Hamas's political strategies. Born in 1956, he led the organization from 1996 to 2017, advocating for Palestinian rights and resistance against Israeli occupation. Mashal has been influential in diplomatic engagements and is recognized for his articulate representation of Hamas's goals on the international stage.

2. Ismail Haniyeh

- Role: Leader of Hamas in the Gaza Strip.

- Background: Born in 1963, Haniyeh assumed various leadership positions within Hamas, including serving as the Prime Minister of the Palestinian National Authority from 2006 to 2014. Known for his role in governance under occupation, Haniyeh has navigated the challenges of leading Hamas in the Gaza Strip.

3. Mahmoud Zahar

- Role: Co-founder and Senior Leader of Hamas.

- Background: Born in 1945, Zahar has been a key figure in the establishment and development of Hamas. With a background in medical practice, he contributed to the early ideological foundations of the organization. Zahar's unwavering stance on resistance and governance has made him a significant voice within Hamas.

4. Yahya Sinwar

- Role: Current Leader of Hamas in the Gaza Strip.

- Background: Born in 1962, Sinwar assumed the leadership role in 2017. With a background as a former prisoner in Israel, he embodies the dual experiences of resistance and political leadership. Sinwar has been noted for his role in shaping Hamas's approach in the Gaza Strip, combining militant resistance with diplomatic engagement.

5. Ismail Radwan

- Role: Senior Hamas Official and Spokesperson.

- Background: As a prominent spokesperson for Hamas, Radwan has been a key communicator of the organization's positions. His role involves articulating Hamas's stance on various issues, including conflicts with Israel and internal Palestinian dynamics.

6. Fathi Hammad

- Role: Former Interior Minister of the Hamas-led government in Gaza.

- Background: Born in 1963, Hammad has held significant positions within the Hamas administration. As Interior Minister, he oversaw security matters in the Gaza Strip. Known for his outspoken rhetoric, Hammad has been a polarizing figure both within and outside of Hamas.

7. Salah al-Arouri

- Role: Deputy Head of Hamas's Political Bureau.

- Background: A significant figure in Hamas, al-Arouri has been involved in various aspects of the organization, including its military wing. Born in 1966, he has played a crucial role in shaping Hamas's strategy, particularly in the context of armed resistance and coordination with other Palestinian factions.

8. Khalil al-Hayya

- Role: Senior Hamas Official and Political Bureau Member.

- Background: Born in 1962, al-Hayya has been actively engaged in political and military aspects of Hamas. With experience in the armed wing of the organization, he transitioned to political leadership. Al-Hayya has been involved in ceasefire negotiations and diplomatic initiatives.

9. Rawhi Mushtaha

- Role: Political Bureau Member and Co-Founder of Hamas.

- Background: A founding member of Hamas, Mushtaha
has been part of the organization since its early days. Born in
1951, he has contributed to shaping the ideological
foundations of Hamas. Mushtaha's role in the political bureau
involves decision-making and strategic planning.

10. Yahya al-Sinwar

- Role: Senior Hamas Official.

- Background: Born in 1962, al-Sinwar has played a
prominent role in Hamas, particularly in military and security
matters. Having spent years in Israeli prisons, he brings both a
personal and strategic perspective to the organization. Al-
Sinwar's leadership role underscores the intersection of
resistance and governance within Hamas.

11. Mousa Abu Marzouk

- Role: Senior Hamas Official and Political Bureau
Member.

- Background: Born in 1951, Abu Marzouk is a seasoned
Hamas leader with extensive experience in political
negotiations. His involvement in diplomatic efforts and
communications has been notable. Abu Marzouk has been a
key figure in representing Hamas in international forums.

12. Hussam Badran

- Role: Former Spokesperson and Member of the Political Bureau.

- Background: Badran, born in 1966, has been a spokesperson for Hamas, articulating the organization's positions to the public and media. His role extends to decision-making within the Political Bureau, contributing to the formulation of strategies and policies.

13. Sami Abu Zuhri

- Role: Former Spokesperson for Hamas.

- Background: Abu Zuhri, born in 1971, served as a prominent voice for Hamas, especially during periods of conflict. As a spokesperson, he played a crucial role in communicating Hamas's positions to the public and the media.

14. Osama Hamdan

- Role: Former Head of Hamas International Relations.

- Background: Hamdan, born in 1965, has been involved in managing Hamas's international relations, navigating the organization's position on the global stage. His diplomatic engagement aimed to garner support for the Palestinian cause and communicate Hamas's perspectives to the international community.

15. Yousef Al-Hasayneh

- Role: Former Minister of Public Works and Housing in the Hamas-led government.

- Background: Al-Hasayneh, born in 1954, assumed a key role in the administration of the Gaza Strip. As Minister of Public Works and Housing, he was tasked with addressing infrastructure challenges and reconstruction efforts in the aftermath of conflicts.

16. Mushir al-Masri

- Role: Senior Hamas Official and Spokesperson.

- Background: Al-Masri, born in 1958, has been a prominent figure in Hamas, serving as a spokesperson and contributing to political discourse. His role involves communicating the organization's positions to the public and the media.

17. Ismail Abu Shanab

- Role: Co-founder of Hamas.

- Background: Abu Shanab, born in 1950, played a foundational role in the establishment of Hamas. His early involvement contributed to shaping the organization's principles and objectives. Tragically, he was assassinated in 2003.

18. Nizar Rayan

- Role: Senior Hamas Leader.

- Background: Rayan, born in 1959, was a senior figure within Hamas, known for his involvement in military and political aspects. He tragically lost his life during the Gaza War in 2009, becoming a symbol of Hamas's commitment to resistance.

19. Ahmed Yassin

- Role: Founder and Spiritual Leader of Hamas (Deceased).

- Background: Yassin, born in 1937, played a foundational role in establishing Hamas in 1987. His leadership provided ideological direction, and he became a prominent figure in the Palestinian resistance. Yassin was assassinated in 2004.

These brief profiles offer a glimpse into the diverse roles and backgrounds of key individuals within Hamas. While some have played crucial roles in shaping the organization's ideology and strategies, others have been pivotal in communicating its positions, managing international relations, and navigating the challenges of governance in the Gaza Strip. Understanding the contributions of these figures provides a nuanced perspective on Hamas's multifaceted engagement in the Israeli-Palestinian conflict.

Chapter 10: Brief Interviews

In the journey through the intricacies of the Hamas-Israel conflict, brief interviews with key figures and analysts serve as invaluable windows into the minds shaping this geopolitical landscape. These snippets capture the essence of perspectives, strategies, and the human side of a conflict that reverberates far beyond borders. From political leaders like Khaled Mashal to diplomatic voices and analysts, these brief interviews offer snapshots, revealing the nuanced dance between resistance and governance, the challenges of diplomacy, and the unyielding pursuit of justice amid a complex geopolitical tapestry. Some of the interviews glimpses are as follow:

Interview with Khaled Mashal, Former Hamas Political Bureau Chief

Journalist: Mr. Mashal, how does Hamas see its role in the conflict with Israel, particularly regarding the strategic decisions made during events like the Gaza War?

Khaled Mashal: Hamas is fundamentally committed to the Palestinian cause, seeking to end the occupation and secure the rights of our people. The Gaza War was a response to the continued Israeli blockade and aggression. Our strategic decisions are rooted in the necessity to defend Palestinians against injustice.

Interview with an Israeli Government Official

Journalist: Israel often cites security concerns when responding to Hamas actions. How does the Israeli government view the prospect of peace and negotiations with Hamas?

Israeli Official: Israel remains committed to achieving peace through negotiations. However, any meaningful dialogue must be based on mutual recognition and a commitment to ending violence. The obstacle lies in Hamas's historic refusal to recognize Israel's right to exist.

Interview with Ismail Haniyeh, Hamas Leader in Gaza:

Journalist: Mr. Haniyeh, how does Hamas balance its dual roles as a resistance movement and a governing body in the Gaza Strip?

Ismail Haniyeh: The dual role is indeed challenging. We govern under the weight of occupation, working to meet the needs of our people. Our resistance activities are driven by the desire to address the root causes of the conflict and secure the rights of the Palestinian people.

Interview with a Palestinian Analyst

Journalist: From a Palestinian perspective, how do you assess the effectiveness of Hamas's approach in light of the broader struggle for statehood?

Palestinian Analyst: Hamas, for some Palestinians, represents a resistance against what is perceived as an unjust occupation. While controversial, their methods resonate with those frustrated by the lack of progress through conventional diplomatic means.

Interview with a Diplomat from an Arab Nation

Journalist: How does your country view its engagement with Hamas, especially considering its designation as a terrorist organization by some?

Diplomat: Our engagement is driven by the belief that inclusive dialogue is essential for regional stability. Designations notwithstanding, we advocate for understanding the root causes of the conflict and addressing them through diplomatic means.

Glossary

1. Hamas: A Palestinian political and militant organization that emerged in the late 1980s. Founded on principles of resistance and the establishment of an independent Palestinian state, Hamas has played a significant role in the Israeli-Palestinian conflict.

2. Israeli-Palestinian Conflict: A long-standing political and territorial dispute between Israelis and Palestinians. Central issues include borders, refugees, control of Jerusalem, and the establishment of a Palestinian state.

3. Gaza Strip: A narrow territory on the eastern coast of the Mediterranean Sea, bordered by Israel and Egypt. Controlled by Hamas since 2007, the Gaza Strip is a focal point of the Israeli-Palestinian conflict.

4. West Bank: A landlocked territory bordered by Jordan to the east and Israel to the west and south. The West Bank is

a core area of contention, housing Palestinian communities and Israeli settlements.

5. Occupation: Refers to the control and military presence of Israel in Palestinian territories, including the West Bank and Gaza Strip. The occupation is a central point of contention in the conflict.

6. Ceasefire: A temporary halt in hostilities agreed upon by conflicting parties. Ceasefires are negotiated to provide relief from violence and create opportunities for diplomatic initiatives.

7. Diplomacy: The conduct of international relations and negotiations between states or organizations. Diplomacy plays a crucial role in seeking resolutions to conflicts such as the Israeli-Palestinian struggle.

8. Two-State Solution: A proposed resolution to the Israeli-Palestinian conflict, advocating for the establishment of

two separate states, Israel and Palestine, living side by side in peace.

9. International Designation: The classification of groups or organizations, such as Hamas, by certain countries or entities as terrorist. Such designations have significant implications for diplomatic engagement and international standing.

10. Root Causes: The underlying historical, political, and social factors contributing to the continuation of the conflict. Understanding the root causes is essential for developing comprehensive solutions.

11. Reconciliation: Efforts to mend internal divisions and conflicts, often referring to attempts to unify Palestinian factions, such as Fatah and Hamas.

12. Qatar and Turkey: Nations that have played intermediary roles in brokering negotiations and ceasefire agreements between Hamas and Israel.

13. Fatah: A major Palestinian political party founded in the 1950s. Fatah has been a key player in Palestinian politics and, at times, has had strained relations with Hamas. It is led by the Palestinian Authority President, Mahmoud Abbas.

14. Cairo Agreement (2011): An agreement aimed at reconciliation between Fatah and Hamas, brokered in Cairo. Despite initial optimism, the implementation of the agreement faced challenges, highlighting the intricate nature of Palestinian internal politics.

15. Legitimacy: The acceptance and recognition of a governing body or organization as lawful and valid. For Hamas, questions of legitimacy arise due to its designation as a terrorist organization by certain entities.

16. Controversy: The state of disagreement and dispute, often surrounding contentious issues. Hamas faces controversy both internationally and domestically, given its dual role as a resistance movement and governing body.

17. Root Causes of the Conflict: Multifaceted historical, political, and social factors contributing to the protracted nature of the Israeli-Palestinian conflict. Understanding these root causes is crucial for addressing the deep-seated issues at the heart of the struggle.

18. International Diplomacy: The engagement of nations and international organizations in negotiations and discussions aimed at resolving conflicts. In the context of the Hamas-Israel conflict, international diplomacy involves efforts to bring about peace and stability.

19. Regional Dynamics: The interactions and relationships between nations in the broader Middle East, influencing the Hamas-Israel conflict. Regional dynamics include the roles played by neighboring countries and international actors.

20. Self-Determination: The right of a people to independently determine their political status, economic development, and cultural identity. The concept of self-determination is central to the aspirations of the Palestinian people.

21. Refugees: Palestinians who were displaced from their homes during the Arab-Israeli wars and their descendants. The status and rights of Palestinian refugees are crucial aspects of the broader conflict.

22. Humanitarian Crisis: Refers to the severe and prolonged deprivation of essential human needs, often resulting from conflict or natural disasters. The Gaza Strip has faced humanitarian challenges, impacting the well-being of its residents.

23. International Recognition: The acknowledgment of the legitimacy and sovereignty of a state or political entity by other nations. The status of international recognition is a key aspect of Palestinian statehood aspirations.

24. Normalization: The process of establishing or improving diplomatic and economic relations between nations. In the context of the Israeli-Palestinian conflict, discussions around normalization often involve the recognition of Israel by Arab states.

25. United Nations (UN): An international organization founded to promote peace, security, and cooperation among member states. The UN has been involved in various resolutions and peace initiatives related to the Israeli-Palestinian conflict.

26. Security Council Resolutions: Decisions made by the United Nations Security Council, which can have binding effects on member states. Several resolutions related to the Israeli-Palestinian conflict have been issued by the Security Council.

27. Arab League: A regional organization of Arab countries, addressing economic, cultural, and political issues. The Arab League has played a role in shaping Arab consensus on matters related to the Israeli-Palestinian conflict.

28. Jerusalem: A city of significance to multiple religions and a focal point of contention in the conflict. Issues related to the status of Jerusalem, including its division and access to holy sites, have been central to negotiations.

29. Settlements: Israeli civilian communities built in the West Bank and East Jerusalem. The construction of settlements is a contentious issue, as it is considered by many as a violation of international law and an obstacle to peace.

30. Refugee Right of Return: The demand for Palestinians displaced during the establishment of Israel to be allowed to return to their homes. This issue is a central point of negotiation and contention in peace talks.

31. Armed Resistance: Refers to the use of military means to resist occupation or achieve political goals. Hamas's armed resistance has been a defining aspect of its strategy in the struggle against Israel.

32. Human Rights Violations: Actions that infringe upon basic human rights, including issues such as restrictions on movement, access to resources, and the use of force against civilians.

33. Non-Governmental Organizations (NGOs): Independent organizations that operate without government affiliation, often involved in humanitarian and advocacy efforts. Numerous NGOs are active in the region, addressing various aspects of the conflict.

34. Water Rights: Disputes over access to and control of water resources, which have been a source of tension between Israel and the Palestinians.

35. Iron Dome: A missile defense system developed by Israel to intercept and destroy short-range rockets and artillery shells. The Iron Dome has played a significant role in mitigating the impact of rocket attacks.

This comprehensive glossary extends the understanding of terms relevant to the Hamas-Israel conflict, encompassing geopolitical, diplomatic, and regional aspects. As the situation continues to develop, staying informed about these terms remains essential for a nuanced comprehension of the ongoing complexities.

Hamas

Understanding a Controversial Organization

Hamas

Understanding a Controversial Organization

Ashu Dhyani

FANTABULOUS

www.fantabulous.co.in

Publisher

Fantabulous Publishers India

www.fantabulous.co.in

Edition

2023

Hamas: Understanding a Controversial Organization

Penned by Ashu Dhyani

Published by Fantabulous Publishers India

Popular Children's Books of the Year ...

My Little Sweet Moon

Haughty Elephant
vs. Cute Rabbit
Vandana Gauniyal

Angel Bird Angelina
Vandana Gauniyal

An Angel In Disguise...
Vandana Gauniyal

Fox Terra and
Crocodile Jambo
Ashish Dhyani

HAUNTED CASTLE
Sneha Pant

A CLEVER FOX SERIES
DUGJA
LION
RETURN

Jolly and Timpu
Best Friends
Kids Story Book
Timpu   Jolly

A Puppy who came for
ice-cream
Geetanjali Pant
Tina   Tuna
Hello everyone

Famous Books of the Year …

Fanta Award Recipient:

(Available in English, Italian, Spanish, French, German and Hindi language.)

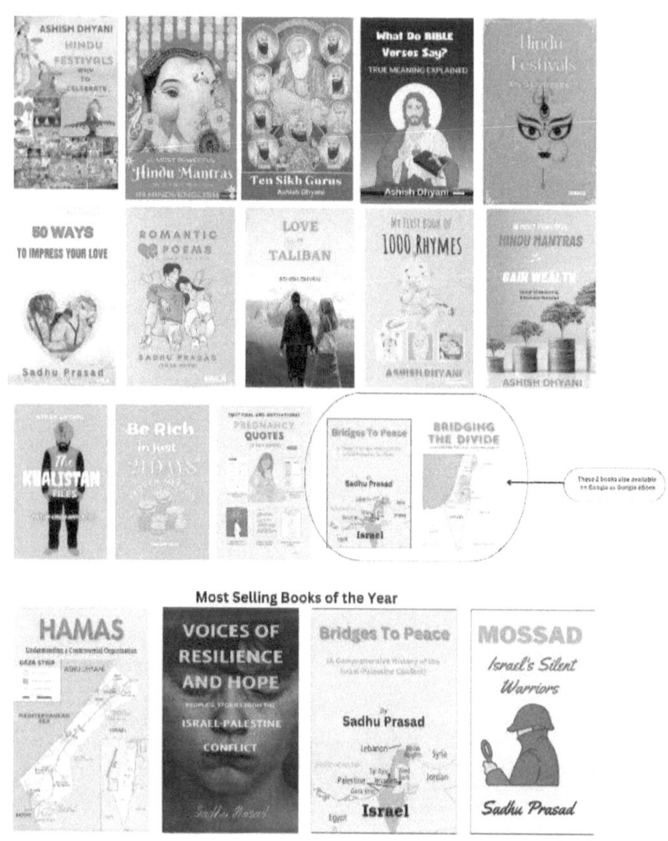

All Books From "Fantabulous Publishers India" Are Available on Amazon-Worldwide.

www.ingramcontent.com/pod-product-compliance
Lightning Source LLC
Chambersburg PA
CBHW021354150726

47989CB00005B/2248